The
Sewing
Machine Guide

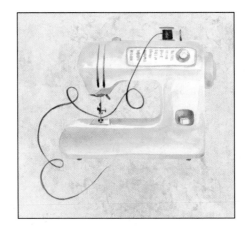

The Sewing Machine Guide

Tips on Choosing, Buying, and Refurbishing

JOHN GIORDANO

The Taunton Press

Taunton
BOOKS & VIDEOS
for fellow enthusiasts

Printed in the United States of America
10 9 8 7 6 5 4 3 2 1

A THREADS Book
THREADS® is a trademark of The Taunton Press, Inc.,
registered in the U.S. Patent and Trademark Office.

The Taunton Press, Inc., 63 South Main Street, PO Box 5506,
Newtown, CT 06470-5506
e-mail: tp@taunton.com

Library of Congress Cataloging-in-Publication Data
Giordano, John.
    The sewing machine guide : tips on choosing, buying, and
refurbishing / John Giordano.
       p.   cm.
    "A Threads book."
    Includes index.
    ISBN 1-56158-220-4
    1. Machine sewing.   2. Sewing machines.   I. Title.
TT713.G56 1997   97-13895
646.2'044—dc21   CIP

Acknowledgments

These companies generously responded to my request for sewing equipment used in the photos: Bernina of America, Elna International, Husqvarna/Viking/White Sewing Machine Co., and Pfaff American Sales.

For the spools of thread in the photos, thanks to American and Efird, Inc.

For permission to photograph their sewing stores, thanks to Creative Sewing Center of Roseville, Minn., and Gratz Sewing Center of Plymouth, Minn.

For the TLC needed to publish this book, thanks to the wonderful staff of the book division of *Threads* magazine.

Special thanks to Mom and Aunt Jane. They can sew anything on any machine, although one likes to and the other doesn't!

Contents

Introduction

On a cold, dark, winter night, you are propped up in a warm, cozy bed thumbing through your favorite sewing magazine. You stop and stare at yet another enticing advertisement for one of those newfangled, do-it-all, top-of-the-line sewing machines and wonder: Could they really be as good as they claim? Is it time to buy one?

You toss. You turn. You dream of repeatable automatic buttonholes, exquisitely embroidered blouses, and quilts to die for.

But wait! Who is that figure hiding in the shadows of your dreamy sewing room? You can hear it whispering: Be careful. This is going to cost a bundle. You should be ashamed of yourself—what's wrong with the old machine? You'll never be able to use it...didn't you say it's computerized? As soon as you pay for it a new model will make yours obsolete. Those dealers will take advantage of you if you give them a chance.

Wake up! Wake up!

I've written this book because making a decision about a wonderful hobby like sewing shouldn't be a nightmare.

I have spent years working with every domestic sewing machine on the market (I currently have 12 of them in my workroom) and have spent a lot of time in sewing-machine stores and sewing-machine repair rooms. That's how I've learned a lot about customers, dealers, sewing machines, the sewing industry, and ways to make sewing more enjoyable. In this book, I'll share the things I have learned so you can make some sensible decisions about one of the most practical, pleasurable, relaxing, and satisfying hobbies on earth: sewing.

In Chapter One, I'll look at sewing and sewing-machine trends and what and why sewers are sewing today. What you sew depends a good deal on your personality, so I'll talk about sewing temperament. See if you fall into any of the categories I've created from my observations of sewers throughout the years.

In Chapter Two, I'll talk about whether you should buy a sewing machine and when. I'll talk about the basics of good decision making, including the difference between making decisions with your brain and with your heart .

In this chapter, I will also discuss the various kinds of sewing machines that are on the market and the pros and cons of the features available—which ones work and which ones don't. The more you know about the products available, the less likely you will make an expensive mistake when it's time for you to buy a machine.

In Chapter Three, I'll discuss how to clean and keep your current machine in good running order. I'll also give you some tips on how to modernize that old machine.

In Chapter Four, I assume that you've decided to buy a sewing machine and have also made some decisions on what kind you want and approximately how much you want to spend.

I'll take you step-by-step through the buying process so that you'll feel comfortable negotiating the purchase of an important part of your creative life. Here you'll find tips on how to find a good dealer, how to negotiate a good price, and how to avoid those "tricks of the trade" that have your mind spinning as the money flies out of your wallet.

In Chapter Five, I'll talk about making the most of your machine after you get it home. I'll share with you some of the things I've learned over the years that can make your investment pay off in productivity and sewing enjoyment. For example, I'll tell you why those tables that are designed "especially for your sewing machine" are the worst things you can buy, and I'll give you some suggestions to improve the accuracy in your sewing.

I hope you enjoy my efforts. Let me know how I've helped, and tell me how you're doing. Drop me a line in care of *Threads* Books, The Taunton Press, Inc., 63 South Main St., PO Box 5506, Newtown, CT 06470. I wish you happy sewing dreams.

CHAPTER ONE

Smart Ways to Think about Sewing

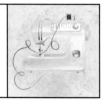

When friends from Europe or South America visit me, they always comment on how inexpensive clothing is here compared to back home. Levi jeans that cost us $30, for example, cost around $100 in Paris. Well, if clothing is that cheap here in the United States, why would people sew, especially if they are busier than ever?

Here's one answer: We have moved away from sewing the necessities of life and have started to sew life's little luxuries.

WHY PEOPLE SEW THESE DAYS

Luxury is a hand-embroidered tablecloth that took Grandma months to cross-stitch. Luxury is the fine hand-sewn buttonhole of a designer dress. Luxury is the monogram on the bath towel or the shirt cuff.

It used to be if you wanted luxury you had two choices: develop the skill to produce the luxury yourself or pay someone big bucks to do it for you. How about you? Do you have the money to buy these luxuries or are you saving for your child's college tuition? Do you have the skill to make your own lace or to hand-sew your buttonholes? And if you *have* the skill, do you have the time to do these things?

Sewing machines to the rescue!

A modern sewing machine can put a lot of luxury into your life very quickly. You can buy a set of rather ordinary napkins and automatically and exquisitely monogram them in a few hours with a sewing machine's embroidery feature. Buy a set of bath towels or a silk blouse and monogram them. Buy a linen suit and embroider your own design on the pocket.

Suddenly the utilitarian sewing machine that made a school uniform, mended a torn blue jean, and made a slipcover for the bedroom chair is now more than ever a versatile tool in the hands of a fabric artist.

As the chart below shows, the world of sewing is changing fast. What will the next trend be? Will quilting continue to be the rage? Will sewing for the home increase as we cocoon? Will a new fabric like Polarfleece change the sewing scene?

Before I discuss choosing and buying a sewing machine, ask yourself which of the following kinds of sewing you do or would like to do. The answers may save you from making a bad choice and wasting a lot of money.

Sewing to save money

Although their number is dwindling, many people still sew to save money, especially if they are sewing upscale clothing. For example, you probably wouldn't save money sewing your own sweat suit because the pattern, fabric, and time would cost you more than buying a good one on sale in any department store. But if you wanted a designer evening dress or a wedding dress, you could probably save a lot of money by making it yourself. You can also save on children's clothing because you need little fabric, and you can build in

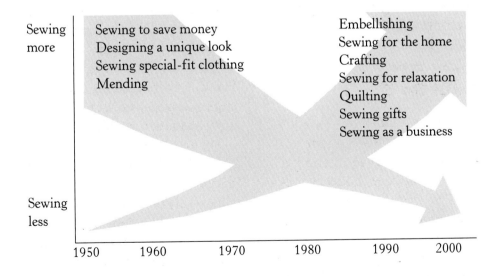

Sewing Trends over the Last 50 Years

Sewing more

Sewing to save money
Designing a unique look
Sewing special-fit clothing
Mending

Embellishing
Sewing for the home
Crafting
Sewing for relaxation
Quilting
Sewing gifts
Sewing as a business

Sewing less

1950   1960   1970   1980   1990   2000

"growth" hems that allow the child to wear the garment longer.

Designing a unique look

My Aunt Jane makes her own clothes because she likes to have control over how she looks. She chooses the fabric, notions, and styles that please her, and she does not limit herself to the choices she finds in department stores. Constructing fine garments from scratch or significantly modifying a pattern requires accomplished sewing and tailoring skills and lots of practice and time. But you'll never find yourself wearing the same dress as the hostess!

Sewing special-fit clothing

Mr. and Ms. Perfect America are the models you see in the advertisement section of the Sunday paper or in the windows of your favorite department stores: The men all have broad shoulders and 30-in. waists, and the women all have perfect figures. Let's face it (and sour grapes be damned): These models are chosen for those ads because they represent what's "average." Well, there are many of us out there with one shoulder higher than the other who know that we don't fit that mold. And that is why we make our own clothes.

Mending

It used to be that people saved money by mending their clothes. When I was in grade school, my grandmother taught me how to reverse my worn and yellowed school-shirt collars to extend the life of the shirt. Nowadays, I don't mend shirts, jeans, or sweats to save money; I mend them because I love them and don't want to throw them out.

Embellishing

More and more people are turning to sewing to embellish and personalize items they construct as well as items they purchase. What used to take Grandma hours of handwork to accomplish can now be done in a flash with the new household computerized sewing and embroidery machines.

Sewing for the home

Sewing well-made drapes and slipcovers is a skill that often requires industrial sewing equipment, special sewing notions (twill tape, rivets, hooks, and rods), and lots of cutting and ironing space. Nonetheless, today homeowners are venturing beyond place mats and napkins to tackle these tricky items as well. There are plenty of books on the market to show you how to make swags, valances, poofs, and Roman shades. And fabric stores have growing departments for home-decor notions.

Crafting

I once worked with a secretary who loved to make rabbit dolls. She spent countless hours creating heirloom outfits for these stuffed creatures, and if you were lucky enough to be in her office at the right time you could buy one of these bunnies for a song and take it home. Other sewers have taken to sewing family crests, seasonal banners to hang from the front porch, wall hangings to hold jewelry, and myriad other items.

Sewing for relaxation

After a difficult day at home or the office, it's nice to lose yourself in a hobby that produces concrete, tangible results. As one woman once told me, "I clean the house all day, but there isn't much to show for it. The family just expects it to be clean, and it always is. But when I sew, I produce something that I can hold on to, that the family is quick to compliment, and that gives me lasting satisfaction. That is why I like to sew."

Some people sew just to relax. They don't quite care what they make, or even if they finish anything, as long as they are sewing. While this may seem pointless to some, these sewers may have discovered an important key to a happy life: Studies have shown that sewing reduces stress.

Quilting

The popularity of quilting has fueled American sewing-machine sales for quite a few years, and now Europeans are catching the quilting bug as well. I'm lucky to be invited to teach a course in international business at a public university in France every year so I get to keep one eye on the sewing world in Europe. Imagine how astonished I was last year to discover that *Le Patchwork* has taken France by storm; every French city has a patchwork store and a patchwork club. It's *trés à la mode*.

Sewing gifts

Calico tops for jam jars, gift bags for bottles of vintage wine, purses, Polarfleece moccasins and gloves, hats, tablecloths, napkins, and ties are all the rage as people turn to personalizing ho-hum gifts. And things are getting pretty personal, too: It seems like the pattern companies can't keep up with the demand from people wanting to sew and give boxer shorts.

Sewing as a business

Micro-sewing studios are springing up all over the country. These aren't businesses that hem pants and skirts and take in seams; they're studios that create, sew, and sell small quantities of unique clothing items. Shoppers are screaming for something different than what is hanging on the racks of every mall in America. The original results of these studios—often sewn on ordinary household machines—are sold at upscale boutiques, art fairs, and church bazaars.

YOUR SEWING TEMPERAMENT

No matter the category, the kinds of sewing you do and do well have a lot to do with your sewing temperament. For example, do you have the patience and skill it takes to do tailoring? Can you stand the repetitive work required by quilting?

Have you ever thought about your sewing temperament? Over the years, I have informally collected observations of my sewing friends, and I find that they fall into several categories. These descriptions are more astrology than science, but you may find that something in them rings true for you. These portraits are intended to get you thinking about your own preferences.

The perfectionist

You are a person who revels in getting things just right and is ready to spend the time it takes to do just that. You love and strive for perfection in your sewing. You like to sew finely tailored and designer clothing, shirts, blouses, and elaborately pieced quilts that all require attention to detail and fine execution.

Your sewing room is a model of efficiency. You buy nothing but the best thread and fabric. You carefully plan your projects and take your time finishing them. When you make a mistake, no matter how small, you undo, rip out, and start again. You are a "foot" person because you understand that precision sewing depends on using the right presser foot. You are skeptical of sergers because they remind you of mass-produced clothing. You will probably never sew the alphabet on your machine. You hand-sew your buttonholes.

You are a fanatic about changing your needle and oiling your machine. Your sewing machine is a high-quality, mechanical, European model with few bells and whistles. You are a good candidate for a commercial machine, which offers speed and many precision feet. You demand perfect straight stitching and consider other stitches concessions to technique.

Like a skilled carpenter, you measure twice and cut once.

Your sewing idol is David Page Coffin.

The quickster

You are emotional, with very little patience and a quick rotary cutter. You always buy much more yardage than you should need because you always seem to need it all. You cut twice and measure once, even though a lot of the time you measure accurately. But since you can't believe you got it right, you cut a second piece just in case.

You have a certain amount of creativity, but you have a hard time managing the relationship between creativity and skill. You have started many projects, but for one reason or another they always wind up as something other than what they started out to be. Some of your projects have been sitting around for a long time, and you are beginning

to cannibalize them to use as those little cutout circles for the tops of your homemade jams and jellies.

Your sewing machine must have variable speed control since your impatience can cause you speedy but poor-quality sewing.

You have limited time so you depend on shortcuts and tricks to make what you want. Your best friends are the rotary cutter and the glue stick. You make unlined jackets, use iron-on interfacing, and like to make sarongs because they require only one pattern piece. You are in love with your serger and use it almost to the exclusion of your sewing machine. However, you turn to the latter when you have to do automatically repeated buttonholes—although deep down you swear you can get away with using Velcro instead of buttons.

You have a high-end sewing machine with all the bells and whistles just in case. Each stitch has its own button. You have no time for embroidery, and your quilts are limited to wall decorations or paper-pattern piecing. Your sewing space, if you can find it, is limited and probably located in your kitchen.

Your sewing idol is Martha Stewart.

Understanding Your Preferences—My Bambi Story

When I was seven, my brother and I begged my mother to buy us the then-wildly popular paint-by-number sets. I'll never forget the trip to the local hobby shop where, much to my displeasure, my brother selected and received a huge kit consisting of large Bambi-in-the-woods scenes, 50 colors, and single-hair brushes for the fine detail work Bambi's eyelashes demanded. I, on the other hand, was limited to much smaller and simpler pictures that required seven or eight colors and two big brushes—not a Bambiesque nuance in sight!

My mother knew me then, as she knows me now, when she said, "You know how you are with these things. You will get them home and finish them in an hour looking to go on to your next project. I'm not going to spend that kind of money on something you won't finish."

Well, she was wrong. Very wrong! I finished those three little pictures of snow-covered wooden bridges in Vermont in 45 minutes, not an hour, and I didn't have any trouble staying within the lines because I completely ignored them. When I was done, my little paint-by-number abstract expressionist works pleased me tremendously, but they only confirmed my mother's assessment of her child's temperament. As she tried to find those little covered bridges hiding in my brilliant paint strokes, she said, "I just don't understand

The creative soul

You are a free spirit with lots of ideas—many, many more than you can sew. You have a large bulletin board covered with clippings. You keep everything because you never know when you'll need it. You are a quilter for sure because the quilt is your canvas; fabric and thread are your media. Since you are incapable of categorizing anything because everything belongs in more than one category, your sewing space appears to be dysfunctional to everyone but you.

Commercial patterns leave you cold, but the Bonfit system that allows you to "design your own" appeals to you. You collect fabric because you love to experiment. In fact, you are currently working on six projects just to see what will happen. You enjoy giving these experiments to others even if they are half finished because you are bored with them.

why you won't make them look like the pictures on the box."

Of course, my brother's Bambi masterpiece took three years to complete, and for that fact alone it deserved the beautiful frame my mother bought. It looked exactly like the picture on the box. (I was promised a similar frame "when you can settle down and follow the instructions.")

That was a long time ago, and my mother is still waiting for me to settle down. But I understand the difference in the temperament between people like my brother and me.

Now don't misunderstand me. I can paint giant Bambi pictures just like the ones on the box, but it bores me to do so. For work and pleasure, I must and do perform tasks that require precision and care, but I much more prefer the creative thinking and experimentation that precedes those events. (Recently, I showed some experimental slashed-fabric swatches to a friend who liked them but had to ask, "What are you going to do with them?" For me, making the swatches was an end in itself. For her, they were just the beginning of a project.)

Understanding your preferences is crucial to achieving success. It helps you to understand and tolerate your limitations, to schedule your time, to reward yourself, and to pick projects and tools that will complement your sewing temperament.

You are definitely a top-of-the-line bells and whistles person. You have every sewing tool imaginable and are a multiple-machine person. You need to jump from project to project, machine to machine, just to keep stimulated. You love all kinds of machines from treadle types to high-end models, and you've got some of your best fabrics folded in piles on top of them. You fall in love with the embellishment possibilities of embroidery machines, but you quickly tire of the prepackaged designs and the hands-off nature of it all. That's not a problem for you because you create your own designs on your computer and sew them out on your top-of-the-line machine.

Your sewing idol is John Giordano.

The cheap and easy-does-it

You have a lot of things on your mind, so any pattern with more than three or four pieces generates confusion. You subscribe to many magazines with the words "Quick and Easy" in their titles. You are not too sure of your sewing skills, but that's all right because you'd rather use glue. You love to make small projects for others. You buy cheap thread. You have been known to put staples in the hems of your dresses and curtains.

Your sewing space is orderly since you have few gadgets—they always break because they are poor quality—and you keep everything in a shoe box. You are addicted to glue guns, iron-on items, pinking shears, and felt.

Your sewing machine was made 20 years ago and is of questionable value. You can't remember when you cleaned it last. When your machine stops functioning you will go to a discount store and replace it with the least expensive model you can find.

You are definitely a candidate for sewing in groups where the coffee and conversation keep you working on your project.

Your sewing idol is…What sewing idol?

Did you see yourself in my sewers' horoscope? I've had fun with these fortune-cookie-like stereotypes, but there is a gram of truth in every fortune cookie. I see bits of myself in all of them, but the creative soul fits me the best. Knowing this, I pick my projects carefully and aim for success and satisfaction instead of frustration and disappointment.

It's important to remember that even if you have a tendency to be like one of the stereotypes I've created, you don't have to be boxed in by it. The thoughtful perfectionist can learn to get a bit wild with a sewing project, and the quickster can complete a big, complicated project if she tackles it in small parts.

When you think about buying a sewing machine, you should take your sewing temperament into account: Do you want a machine that matches your temperament or one that challenges it? Do you want a machine that makes you better at what you already do or one that allows you to add something new to your menu of sewing skills?

And finally, does your budget match your sewing temperament? For example, if you are a perfectionist but only have $300 to spend, what kind of machine should you buy?

What you want to sew should be compatible with what kind of sewer you are.

CHAPTER TWO

Smart Ways to Choose a Sewing Machine

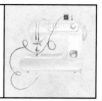

Sewing relaxes me. Buying a sewing machine doesn't.

I spend a lot of time testing new and used sewing-machine models and hanging out in sewing-machine shops talking to the salespeople, owners, and technicians. While doing this, I've watched many a customer come in to a shop and agonize over whether or not she should buy a sewing machine and which machine it should be. Was she making a mistake? Was she getting a good deal?

Why, I've wondered, are we so uptight about buying a machine when sewing itself is such a relaxing pastime?

And then it hit me: It's like buying a car. Once you drive it out of the showroom, it's yours. It's like using a computer. The silly, little appliance you are trying to boss around seems to know more than you do. It's like selecting a musical instrument. The right one will help you to express your creativity; the wrong one will just frustrate you. It's like getting married. You always wonder how your life would have been different if you had selected the other model.

Choosing and buying a sewing machine is complicated because it involves spending big money, dealing with new technology, knowing the limits of your creativity, and understanding your own ego.

I understand because I've been there.

THE STRATEGY OF CHOOSING

Whenever I am faced with a difficult sewing-machine buying

A Sad Sewing Story with a Happy Ending

I once fell in love with a sewing machine that I had to have. I saved up my dollars to buy it, and when they totaled $2,300, I bought it. (The asking price was $2,900. See pp. 76-79 on bargaining techniques.) I took it home and found myself immediately disappointed and depressed with my purchase. Yes, I had studied all the models. Yes, I wanted *that* machine. Yes, it was a well-deserved birthday present to myself. So why was I so unhappy?

When I think about that purchase, I now realize that I was caught in a conflict between my head and my heart. I wanted that machine. After all, didn't I deserve a great present for my birthday? Yet I felt guilty spending that kind of money. Since I couldn't live with the conflicting emotions, I asked the dealer to take the machine back. He wouldn't. So, I placed an ad in the paper and sold it for $300 less than I paid.

The moral of the story is a $300 mistake is cheaper than a $2,300 mistake.

I don't regret selling that machine. I would have never been happy with it. (A few weeks later at a garage sale, I bought a wonderful Bernina 310 for $10 and spent a most satisfying week making it purr again.)

If decisions like spending several thousand dollars for a sewing machine are difficult for you to make, or if you are like me and you sometimes make decisions now only to regret them later, you may want to think about how you make decisions in the first place.

decision, I ask myself three crucial questions:
- Can I really afford this purchase?
- Do I need, want, or deserve this machine?
- Are my head and my heart together in this decision?

Let me give you some strategies for answering each.

Can I afford this purchase?

Since a sewing machine is not usually returnable to the dealer for a refund, it is important to ask this question concerning your hard-earned money up front: Can I afford to buy a new machine?

If you come to the conclusion that you really can't afford to buy a sewing machine at this time, don't despair. On pp. 68-70 I give you

10 creative ways to find the "hidden" money in your life. If you can't save the money on your own, your sewing-machine dealer might have a payment plan to help you out.

Do I need, want, or deserve this machine?

In my favorite kitchenware shop, I stood in front of a wonderful electric ice cream maker that makes a quart of ice cream in a half hour. Just add the ingredients, push the button, and wait. It costs $499. Oh yes, I wanted it. I wanted it badly. I'd even promised myself that I would only make low-calorie sherbets with it, *not* those delicious, creamy, custard-based ice creams with names like espresso-cream-nut-swirl—yes!—with a dab of chantilly and a cherry on top.

It's at delicate moments like this that I ask myself some important questions: Is this something I really need or is it something I really want? And finally, do I deserve this?

Is there any question in your mind that I *wanted* that ice cream machine? There wasn't in mine. So why didn't I buy it? When I thought about what that ice cream would do to my arteries and my waistline, I knew beyond any doubt that I didn't *need* that machine.

Did I deserve this machine? This is the hard part. For better or for worse, "deserve" for me is connected to "What have you done lately?" If I finish this book on time, I deserve a treat. If I lose 30 pounds, I deserve X. If I get good grades, I deserve Y. Well, that's how I motivate myself. How about you?

I didn't buy that ice cream maker because after thinking about it for a long while, I hadn't really done anything special lately to *override* the negative "need" vote.

So what about this sewing machine you want so much that you dream about it? Do you really need it? Did you do anything special lately to deserve it?

On a scrap of paper, write down some sentences about why you want, need, and deserve a sewing machine. Then, if possible, put these statements in your desk drawer for a day or two and relax. When you reread them, do your statements show you a clear decision-making path?

The chart on p. 16 gives some examples to help you. You may find the same example in more than one category, but that's because a "want" for me may be a "need" for you. Don't worry about that; just do the exercise.

Want, Need, Deserve

Want	Need	Deserve
• I want what Jane has.	• I need a machine that can do heavy-duty work.	• I deserve a new toy for reaching my personal (financial, health, business) goals.
• I want to do embroidery.	• I need a machine that will last 20 years.	• I deserve a reward for saving money by making my own clothes.
• I want a high-quality machine.	• I need a machine that sews leather.	
• I want a machine that will allow me to experiment.	• I need a machine that can memorize and repeat a sewing task.	• I deserve a machine that will respond to my creative needs.
• I want all the attachments.	• I need a machine to mend clothes.	• I deserve a machine equal to the value of my husband's golf clubs.
• I want a machine that has a lot of fancy stitches.	• I need a machine that is easy to carry around.	• Your statement:
• I want a machine that sews sideways.	• Your statement:	
• I want an industrial machine.		
• Your statement:		

Are my head and my heart together in this decision?

When you think about buying something for yourself, does your mind tell you one thing and your heart another? This happens to all of us as we internally "discuss" the pros and cons of making any purchase. Here is a nonsewing example to illustrate the point: For years the graduate students in my international management course have asked my advice on what language they should study.

Oftentimes, I can plainly see that they are caught between the conflicting messages they are receiving from their heads and from their hearts. "I should study Spanish because I know that will help me the most. But I'm not sure." When I ask the students what their hearts are telling them, they may choose German because they remember eating delicious kuchen at their German grandma's house.

Write down some head statements and some heart statements about

Some Head and Heart Responses

Buy a machine?	Head response	Heart response
Yes	• This machine will pay for itself. • I've saved up a long time for this; it is time to buy. • I'm going to use this for a special project. • Your statement:	• I deserve this treat. • I've always wanted a fine new machine. • I love the way this machine looks and feels. I just want it. • Your statement:
No	• This is too rich for my budget. • My old machine works just fine. • I don't have enough information to make a good decision yet. • Your statement:	• I'm afraid I'll make a mistake and get stuck with something I don't like. • I feel guilty spending so much money on myself. • I love the machine I have now. • Your statement:

buying a sewing machine. The chart above gives some statements to get you started, but be sure to add your own. Again, put them away for a few days and go back to them with fresh eyes.

What is your tendency? Do you always seem to make decisions based on what your heart tells you only to wind up paying too much for something that doesn't work right? Or do you always seem to make decisions based on what your head tells you only to have something that works right but doesn't really make you happy?

If most of your thoughts and statements about buying a sewing machine fall into the "yes" part or the "no" part of the chart, you have a clear basis on which to make a decision. If, on the other hand, you are like me, you will find that some of your statements fall into seemingly contradictory categories. This is normal.

My friends who study Zen wonder why I am so determined to separate the head and the heart; they tell me that I am talking about one and the same thing! Perhaps the real trick is to balance the two. No matter, I now know beyond a doubt that making a decision with my heart isn't going to make me happy if I ignore what my head tells me.

DECIDING TO BUY A SEWING MACHINE

Even though the marketplace is getting more complicated, making a decision about whether or not to buy a sewing machine and what kind to buy need not be a life-arresting dilemma. In the chart on the facing page, I've turned the process into a little stroll along a path. All you have to do is answer a question every time you come to a fork in the path. "Yes" will take you in one direction, and "no" will take you in the other. Start in the upper left corner of the path. If you find the question difficult to answer, just turn to the page indicated on the chart for a discussion of that topic.

If you've decided to keep the machine you already have, I'm going to tell you how to take care of it and even how to modernize it for greater sewing convenience (see pp. 33-49).

If you've decided to keep your machine and buy another one, you should read the section on how to put your old machine in good order (see pp. 33-44) and the section on how to buy another (new or used) machine (see pp. 66-81).

If you've decided to buy a used machine, I have some great pointers and some suggestions on what models to look for (see pp. 52-54).

And if you've decided to buy a new machine, I'm going to tell you how to buy the right one at the right price (see pp. 76-81).

But first, a few words on sewing machines in general.

Should You Buy a Sewing Machine?

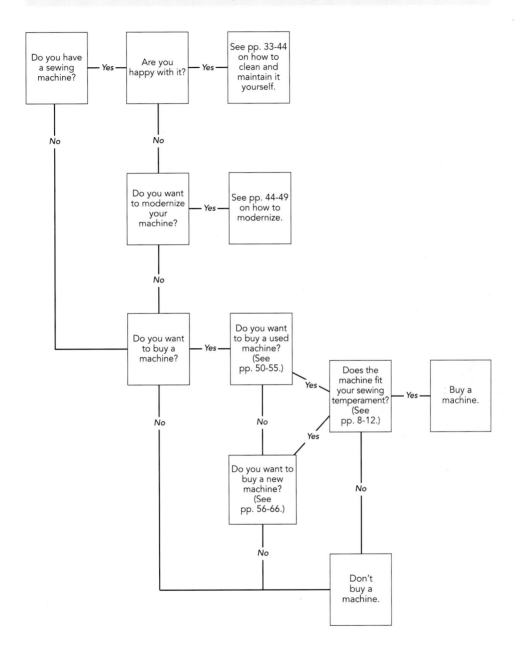

This New Home household machine is a low-end mechanical model that can sew about a dozen stitches and a no-turn buttonhole. The accessory case has been removed to show the free arm for sewing cuffs and tubes.

A household plus embroidery machine, this computerized, mid-range Husqvarna Viking model named The Rose goes from a regular machine with 40 stitches and automatic buttonhole to one that does hooped-fabric embroidery at the touch of a button.

KINDS OF SEWING MACHINES

I assume that you are considering buying a new or used household sewing machine, but there are other categories of machines out there. Here are some of the categories of sewing machines on the market today.

Regular household

This is the multipurpose machine most of us have or want. It is probably the most complicated home appliance you can buy. Not only must it sew a straight seam but it must also do decorative work, make buttonholes, and mend as well. Newer, computerized machines may include sideways sewing and the ability to connect to your home computer so you can create your own stitches and embroidery designs.

Household plus embroidery

This is the most popular upper-price-point machine on the market today. It includes all of the features of the regular model mentioned above, plus automatic hooped embroidery.

Household embroidery

This machine does only embroidery and is meant to be a companion to your regular household machine. Some people like this two-machine strategy, as it allows them to sew on one machine while the embroidery machine is running, often for longer than 15 minutes.

Light commercial

This mechanical machine is designed for multipurpose, heavy-duty use, for instance, in a tailor's shop or at a dry cleaner. There are very few of them on the market. Some home sewers like this machine because it offers some of the versatility of the home machine, but it also sews at greater speeds and is more substantial than a household machine.

Industrial machines

This machine is designed for task-specific (buttonholes, chain stitch, or leather), repetitive sewing at very high speeds. Most machines of this type are still purely mechanical all-metal workhorses, but new machines now come with computerized counters and other features like stitch memory that makes repetitive sewing almost automatic. Modern industrial machines can remember and repeat

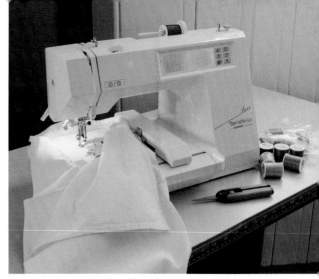

This mid-range Bernette made for Bernina, called the Deco 500, is a household embroidery machine dedicated to hooped embroidery. After you insert a design card, you touch the screen to make your choice.

Industrial machines like this Bernina 217 N (shown at right) are set into heavy-duty tables under which sits the large, powerful motor. The machine on the left is a light commercial Bernina 950, which also fits into a table like the one shown.

a specific pattern of sewing, like the number of stitches it takes to sew a pocket onto a shirt. The operator simply turns the fabric when the machine stops and automatically lifts the presser foot. These heavy machines are set in special tables and are linked by a belt to a separate, high-speed motor. Some home sewers like their speed, quality of stitch, and smooth, uncomplicated operating features. See the sidebar on the facing page to see if you should buy an industrial machine.

Commercial embroidery

Usually attached to a computer, this is the multithread, multineedle machine you see in shopping malls that embroiders names on baseball hats, T-shirts, and towels. Some entrepreneurial sewers have purchased these costly machines and started small home businesses.

Household serger

Popular in the last 10 years, this is the machine that cuts and sews an overlock stitch at the same time. Like the household sewing machine, it is a multipurpose machine that offers chain stitching; two-, three-, four-, or five-stitch overlocking; and cover stitching. Sewers like the speed with which they can simultaneously cut and bind fabric with this machine. A serger can be a companion to a sewing machine but cannot replace it. See the chart on p. 24 and the sidebar on p. 25 for a comparison of the two.

Industrial serger

This heavy-duty machine is designed to serge day in ad day out. Like the industrial sewing machine, it is set into its own table and is connected by a belt to a high-speed motor. If you assemble a lot of knits, this may be the machine for you.

TYPES OF HOUSEHOLD SEWING MACHINES

Although the market is changing slightly—sales of industrial machines to home sewers is increasing—it is nonetheless true that most sewers buy household models. It used to be that the only difference between sewing machines was the color...and they were all black. Until recently, there wasn't a significant difference in what sewing machines could do: a zigzag stitch was a zigzag stitch was a zigzag stitch. Mostly what you shopped for was quality of stitching and ease of use.

Should You Buy an Industrial Machine?

There are a few industrial or commercial machines on the market that might interest you if you are willing to sacrifice variety and versatility for speed and accuracy. Basically what I am talking about is sewing on a machine like Grandma's old, black, straight-stitch Singer...only it's on steroids!

What you do get is beautiful straight stitching (and in a few cases zigzag capability as well) and astounding sewing speed. Sewing accuracy is improved by a few important characteristics of these industrial monsters: They are always flatbed machines set into a large table so you have plenty of support for your sewing project. And the speed itself allows you to sew more accurately since you don't have time to wiggle the fabric around as when the poky household machine makes its

stitches. The feet on industrial machines are well made to stand constant use, and they don't jiggle as snap-on feet often do. The result is more accurate feeding of the fabric and more accurate sewing.

The bad news is that industrial machines do not come with the built-in fun that the top-of-the-line household machines do; they are designed for no-nonsense, task-oriented business applications. You can't switch stitches at the touch of a button, you won't find dozens of decorative stitch choices, and you won't be able to automatically sew buttonholes.

The bobbin on an industrial machine is actually smaller than on some household machines. The machine is very heavy and not portable. It requires its own special table, which is usually, but not necessarily, sold with the

machine, and you need to leave the table in one place. The motor is under the table and attached to the machine by a belt, just like the old treadle machine. If you choose the clutch motor, it runs constantly when you turn the machine on, even if you aren't sewing. A standard motor, which is quiet until you step on the "gas," is better for home sewers, but the good ones are more expensive than the clutch type.

If you mostly construct clothing and do very little machine embellishment or if you have plenty of room in your studio for more than one machine, an industrial model might become your main machine, leaving embellishment and buttonholes to its domestic sister. Visit your industrial-machine dealer and test the industrial type the way you would any other sewing machine.

Sewing Machines vs. Sergers

Sewing machine	Serger (overlock machine)
Very easy to thread and to choose various stitches. Easy to use.	Very difficult to thread and to change from one stitch to another. Once threaded or converted, it is easy to use.
Easily sews in the middle of fabric as well as on the edges.	Sews mostly on the edges of fabric. Chain stitch and cover stitch are possible in the middle of fabric, but you must convert the machine to do this.
Needle can be fixed (for straight stitch) or move sideways depending on the pattern selected. Feed dogs move the fabric forward, backward, and, on newer, top-of-the-line machines, sideways.	Needles are in fixed positions. Feed dogs move the fabric forward only. On some models, two sets of feed dogs, which are independently set, control the movement of the fabric—this is called differential feed. If one is set slower than the other, you can create ruffles or reduce puckering in some fabrics.
Top thread and bobbin thread produce a stitch. The stitches lock. You have to rip out the stitches to undo.	Three to five threads produce a nonlocking stitch (something like crochet or knitting), which can unravel if you pull on the right thread.
Cannot cut fabric.	Can cut fabric while it overlocks an edge—one of the serger's strong points.
Modest thread use with straight stitch. Narrow range of decorative threads determined by eye of needle.	Uses lots of thread. Wide range of threads are possible in loopers that have larger eyes than needles.
Bobbin thread must be replaced often.	There is no bobbin thread. Large cones of thread last a long time.
Sews up to 900 stitches per minute.	Sews very fast—up to 1,700 stitches per minute.

Should You Buy a Serger?

Many books have been written to introduce sergers to the home sewer, mostly to answer the questions: What is it? What does it do? Do I need one?

Here's my short version of this book: Your sweat suit was serged. The pocket on your blouse was sewn. Compare the stitches.

A sewing machine and a serger are like a hammer and a screwdriver. Both are tools, but both do very different things (see the chart on the facing page).

Strictly speaking, all of your sewing can be done on a regular sewing machine. But just as machine sewing is less time-consuming than hand sewing, sergers make many sewing tasks much easier for the busy sewer. These tasks include cutting and binding edges at the same time, making rolled hems on sheer fabrics, and joining stretch knits.

In my opinion, a serger is useful after you learn how to sew well. Entirely serged garments have the same caché as sweat suits, but a well-sewn garment can benefit from a serger-finished seam.

If you can afford only one, buy a sewing machine. If you can afford both, think about buying them at the same time to get a good price.

Quality and ease of use are still important today, but there are many more variables for the sewer to consider. You can still buy a basic machine, but you can also buy one that does everything but scrub the kitchen sink. Here's some information on the variations of household machines available on the market today.

Mechanical machines
Today, the very earliest sewing machines seem like toys to us, since they were so tiny and simply

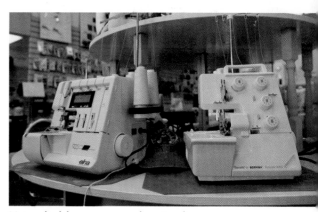

Household sergers can be simple or complex. The computerized, high-end Elna 925 (left) has it all, while the simpler Bernette FunLock 006D does the basics.

I bought each of these for less than $10 at secondhand stores. The flatbed Brother shown in the back has dual voltage. The Bernina 717 (left) came with an extension table. The New Home machine (right) cost $5 because its accessory box was missing.

When you sew on this lightweight, quiet electronic Elna Carina, the needle always stops out of the fabric. The black disks shown at left are the cams you insert to sew various decorative and utility stitches.

constructed. You turned a wheel with your right hand and guided the fabric through the machine with your left—I have a child's Singer that works just like that. And in parts of the world where there is no electricity, that's the way it is still done. Imagine how excited people became when they discovered that foot power could run a treadle machine and free both hands. Eventually, a small motor replaced foot power, but the machine remained basically the same.

In the 1950s, mechanical machines became as complicated as Swiss clocks and were made of just as many (thousands of) parts. The machines could sew zigzag and straight stitches, and with the use of built-in or inserted cams they could produce decorative motifs as well. Some of these beautiful machines are still being made today, but they are a fast-dying breed because they are too costly to manufacture and don't meet the more sophisticated expectations of today's computer-savvy sewer.

Electronic machines

In the 1970s, electronic circuit boards were added to the electric systems of sewing machines that would send maximum power to the motor at any speed—a great and useful innovation. When you are sewing jeans, for example, you may want to sew slowly, but you also want maximum needle-penetrating power. This is impossible on a purely mechanical machine because the harder you step on the pedal, the more power you send to the motor and the faster it sews. If, however, you step lightly on the pedal, you send less power to the motor and that's when you get into trouble on thick fabrics.

Electronics also allows the needle to always stop up or down (in or out of the fabric), and sometimes you can choose. Some machines even have an electronic eye that "reads" the plastic bobbin to tell you when thread is getting low. Nonetheless, the machine remains basically the same sewing instrument as the mechanical model, especially concerning stitch selection. The machines still depend on internal or user-inserted cams to be "read" by a mechanical finger to produce various patterns.

Computerized machines

A sewing machine containing a computer chip doesn't depend on a cam to give you a pattern. A pattern is written into the brain of the

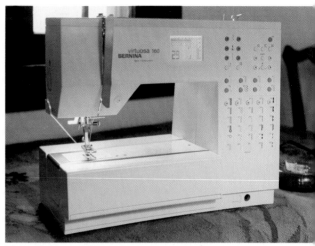

This mid-range Bernina Virtuosa 160 has a computer on board. Push a button and the machine automatically sets the appropriate length and width for the stitch selected.

machine by a computer programmer. All you need to do is call up the pattern, usually by dialing its address. For example, you push the "2" button and the "4" button to get stitch recipe number 24. A computer can also remember the things you tell it to do and repeat those things on command.

Imagine sewing one buttonhole and telling your sewing machine to remember what you've just done. Now tell your machine to repeat that buttonhole automatically, over and over again. Yes, this is possible with a computerized machine.

A Word about Hardware, Software, and Interface

Don't be intimidated by computer language when you go to look at a computerized sewing machine; it's really not all that complicated. Hardware is the sewing machine itself; it's what you feel when you pick it up and what breaks when you drop it. Hardware is the motor and parts that make the needle go up and down to make stitches.

Software is the invisible-to-you, automatic instruction given to the sewing machine to do the work. For example, the software tells the hardware (the needle) to move in a certain way to make a certain stitch. And software is what tells the machine how to embroider a bunch of cherries on your favorite dress.

A good sewing machine must have both good hardware and good software to function properly. A weak motor, badly configured metal or plastic parts, and poor engineering will not give you good stitches or make sewing enjoyable. Usually the more expensive the machine, the better the hardware inside.

An expensive, well-made machine filled with inaccurate computer instructions is not any good either. It is the computer that tells the needle where and when to sew, so sloppy computer instructions are not a sewer's friend. I have worked on computerized sewing machines that do some strange and aggravating things, and there was no way to change the machine's behavior until the manufacturer upgraded the memory chip. It's a good idea not to run out and buy a newly introduced model in order to give the manufacturer time to work the bugs out. The good news for American sewers is that the bugs are often discovered in the home market, such as Switzerland, Germany, Japan, or Sweden, so the machines are relatively reliable when they get here.

Interface was a sewing word long before it was a computer word. Interface is something that you put between two things that connects them. In sewing, it's a layer of fabric between two other layers, and in the computer world, it is what allows you to communicate in plain English to a computer that only understands the language of zeros and ones.

But we don't have to talk about computers to understand the impor-tance of interface. Even a TV from the 1950s had it: Where were the dials placed? Were the numbers and labels easy to read? Were the controls arranged in a logical order?

Interface is the con-nection between you and the machine. Even if the machine has good hard-ware and good software, it should also be friendly to use—easy for you and the machine to "talk" to each other. Unclear instructions, poorly placed buttons and levers, and complicated and poorly lit screens filled with jumbled information are going to make sewing difficult.

It is also logical that an interface good for one person may not be good for another. For example, if you are an older sewer with declin-ing eyesight and some hand-coordination prob-lems, you may not do well with a sewing machine with tiny buttons placed close together. If you are sen-sitive to high pitches, some of the machines with shrill audio beeps may drive you crazy.

Here's my quick, guide to getting a happy inter-face on your new sewing machine: Try it before you buy it. What makes good sense to a sewing-machine engineer in the factory isn't necessarily going to make a whole lot of sense to you.

Mechanical parts that were once linked with belts and gears can now be run by separate computer-responsive motors. When you push a pattern button (or touch the screen itself on some models) on a computerized machine, the brain coordinates the needle position with the hook, the feed dog, and, in some machines, the tension mechanism.

Even in less expensive computerized sewing machines, the stitch library will be surprisingly extensive and built in. In the more expensive models, you can add to your stitch library by buying more patterns that come on credit-card-sized computer cards that you slide into the machine. It's just like buying software programs for your computer.

If you like the idea of creating your own stitches but don't have a computer or a computer-connectable sewing machine, Bernina or Pfaff may have a computerized machine to suit you. A small device called the Creative Designer attaches to a Pfaff 7670 or 7570 model to let you draw and enter into the sewing machine any 9mm stitch you want. The Bernina model 1630 has a built-in track ball that lets you draw a pattern on the screen of the sewing machine. The machine then sews the pattern at your choice of five different widths. On both machines, creating stitches is something easy and fun to do.

Because they require fewer parts, are easier to manufacture, and offer the sewer greater options and ease of use, computerized machines have started to replace mechanical ones. In a few years, the mechanical sewing machine will take its place next to the black-and-white TV.

Computer-connectable machines

While some sewers are satisfied with a few stitches, some want them all. So they buy a machine that accepts computer cards (or keys) that increase the patterns and stitches their machine can produce.

But some sewers don't want to be limited to the stitches offered by the manufacturer; they want to create their own.

You *can* create your own stitches on some top-of-the-line sewing machines because they attach to your home computer. You can draw or paint an original design on your computer and send it directly or via memory cards to your sewing machine to be stitched. You can even scan images into the computer with an optional piece of equipment,

Closed- and Open-System Sewing Machines

Both mechanical and computerized machines can be closed or open systems.

In a closed-system machine, you cannot add to the patterns offered. With a closed-system machine, you will *always* be limited to the built-in stitches. If that's all you need or want, fine. You won't be spending any more money on your sewing machine.

In an open-system machine, there are some built-in stitches, but you can also add to the selection by inserting a cam or a computer chip card or key. With an open-system machine, you can keep adding new stitches as they become available. You can't have enough of these designs and they often cost plenty. The cost of collecting optional stitches and patterns might even be greater than buying the machine itself!

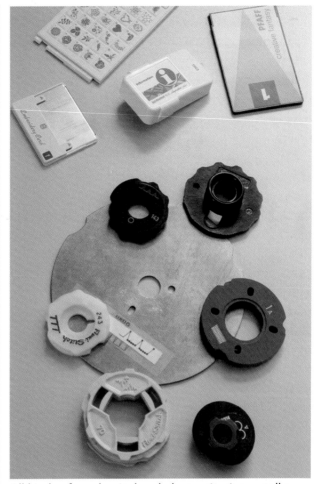

All kinds of mechanical and electronic gizmos tell an open-system sewing machine what stitch to sew. Each of the cams in the foreground represents one stitch, while the electronic cards and keys in the background contain dozens of designs. The big brass cam is for an industrial machine.

separate the colors, and tell the machine to stitch each color separately.

If you like computers and you want to sew a motif that no one in the world has but you, then this expensive option might be for you.

WHICH KIND OF SEWING MACHINE IS FOR YOU?

The kind of machine you should buy depends on what you sew. A mechanical machine may be all you need for making curtains, clothing, or quilts. On the other hand, if you want automatic embroidery, you have no choice: The computerized machine is the only one that can store, recall, and execute those complicated designs.

I don't particularly care how computers work, I just like what they do...most of the time. When you sew on a computerized machine, it has a different feel than a mechanical one because there are several motors and the computer brain is telling them what to do. It does take some getting used to.

With the mechanical models, you feel that the machine is connected to your foot, which is connected to *your* brain. The harder you press down, the faster the machine goes, but when you take your foot off the pedal, the machine may sew an extra stitch or two as it slows to stop (electronic and computerized models usually come to an abrupt stop).

There is something smooth and satisfying about mechanical machines when they are running well, but I have to admit that I enjoy the benefits of computerization too, which is why I have more than one machine.

CHAPTER THREE

Smart Ways to Maintain Your Sewing Machine

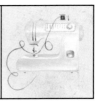

Before you decide to buy a new sewing machine, you may want to consider keeping the one you have, for several reasons.

First, not all old machines are useless. In fact, some of them make better stitches than newer machines. Second, keeping, cleaning, and possibly repairing the machine you have will be much cheaper than buying a new one. Finally, you can give your old machine some modern features by using some of the tricks and ideas that follow.

If you decide to keep your machine, start by cleaning it to get it into top-notch running condition.

HOW TO CLEAN AND REPAIR THE MACHINE YOU HAVE

A sewing machine is the most complicated appliance you have in your home. While it is not nearly as complicated as a car, no matter what brand or age machine you have, it requires regular internal and external inspection for possible cleaning, lubrication, replacement of parts, and other preventative maintenance.

Perhaps it is stretching a point to compare a sewing machine to a car (both have a motor, belts, gas pedal, gears, lights), but I find that many sewers have the same attitude toward both: You want it to get you there, but you don't care how it works. Well, you don't have to know how your car works to understand that you must change the oil and clean the air and gas filters once in a while. Doing so will prolong any car's life and keep it running smoothly.

It is easy and economical to take good care of your sewing machine—much easier and cheaper than taking care of your car, that's for sure. By cleaning your machine yourself, you will save the typical $39.95 dealers charge for a "tune-up" and double the life of your machine. Keep that

$40 (and the fabric it can buy) in mind as you read the following sections; it helps to make a potentially tedious topic a lot more interesting.

Why and when to clean and oil

You must clean your sewing machine to keep it free of dust, grit, and gummy grime, like that caused by cigarette smoke or poor-quality or inappropriate sewing-machine oil. All of these materials act like sandpaper and glue, resulting in the machine's poor sewing performance and, ultimately, shortening its life.

Enter enough grit, gum, heat, and friction and the machine stops dead.

When metal rubs against metal, the result is friction and heat, wear and tear, and, finally, poor performance or breakdown. You must oil your sewing machine, but not the motor, to keep the parts moving if the manufacturer recommends doing so. (Most older machines and some new ones require oiling, but some are designed to be self-lubricating, and it is a mistake to oil them. Check the manual that came with your machine.)

Many of today's sewing-machine manufacturers have replaced metal parts with plastic ones for sensible reasons: plastic is lighter and cheaper than metal, of course. And certain kinds of plastic—nylon, for instance—are self-lubricating and very tough. But plastic is more susceptible to grit, and it doesn't have the expansion and contraction properties of metal, so it can crack.

While cleaning and oiling are sewing-machine maintenance twins—things that you usually perform at the same time—they are really very different tasks: cleaning takes out the grit; oiling lubricates. You take out the grit before you put in the oil.

Inspecting the machine

There is an important difference between "repair" and "inspect and clean." Few of us are prepared to repair sophisticated mechanical equipment ourselves, and I don't think we should. But, with a bit of guidance, all of us are capable of inspecting and cleaning any piece of household machinery. We do it all the time with typewriters, vacuum cleaners, refrigerators, stoves, irons, and, when push comes to shove— my personal nemesis—cars.

Even though the tools I use are simple household items, I like to have everything at hand when I start inspecting a machine. It's easier to find objects on brown paper, although newspapers will also work.

To inspect a machine, set it on brown paper, newspapers, or carpet squares (to keep tools and screws from rolling around) on a well-lit, sturdy, flat surface (see the photo above). I use the kitchen table. Have your tools within reach. Unthread the machine and remove the needle, foot, and bobbin.

Plug in the machine, step lightly on the gas pedal and listen. Yes, close your eyes and listen. A "healthy" machine runs quietly, is clink- and tick-free, and is relatively free of vibration, especially at

An ordinary egg carton is perfect for holding needles, small parts, and the oiler when cleaning the machine. A plastic ice-cube tray is a good substitute.

modest speed. Machines with rotary hooks, where the hook goes continuously around, usually sound quieter than oscillating ones, where the hook goes back and forth. Also, more expensive models should sound quieter than cheaper ones. The machine shouldn't sound like your electric mixer when you ask it to handle too much cookie dough. When you buy a new or reconditioned machine, close your eyes and memorize its "healthy" sound. You'll quickly be able to tell when your machine needs help if and when the sound changes.

The machine shouldn't hesitate to start when you step on the accelerator. If the motor hums, strains, and hesitates, and then the machine takes off rapidly, the machine probably needs to be lubricated. Complete the inspection and cleaning process as I recommend, and you may find that the machine will be more responsive.

Don't run a machine that makes loud noises or clicks or that shows a lot of resistance to the motor; there may be a serious problem. Unplug the machine and take it to the repair shop.

Cleaning the upper level of the machine

Before going "under the hood," take a moment to inspect and clean some of your machine's important external parts.

- Clean the thread spoolholders and replace the circle felt pads if worn. The pads keep the spool turning smoothly and prevent clattering.
- Clean the thread-tension discs and bobbin-winder spring with a soft cloth dipped in some rubbing alcohol.
- Clean the outside "skin" of the machine with a soft cloth sprayed with a household cleaner.
- If the motor belt and bobbin rubber ring are worn, buy replacements at any hardware store.
- If there are nicks in the needle plate, buy a replacement plate at any sewing-machine repair shop.

Now let's go inside. There are one to four servicing entrances on most machines: the needle-and-light door, the lid, the bobbin-mechanism door, and the bottom-of-the-machine door (see the photos on p. 38). First open the needle-and-light door, which is the left-hand door just above the needle, if there is one. It usually hinges open to the left, snaps off, or is held in place with a single screw. Put the screws and all the parts you remove in an egg carton or ice-cube tray, where they will be easy to find and differentiate when reassembling.

Now take off the lid (check your manual to see if the manufacturer indicates maintenance points here; some newer machines don't). Usually there are one or two screws holding the lid in place. Unscrew them (they can be very long), and gently jiggle the lid a little to see which way it comes off. Some lids slide, some clip on, some are hinged, and some just fall off.

Once the needle-and-light door and lid are off or open, you can look inside. Do not panic. You are *not* going to do anything here but inspect and clean. Relax, you don't need the screwdriver any more. Now take a deep breath and a good look.

Some machines have just a few parts, while others, like the sophisticated mechanical ones built in the '50s and '60s, are often very complicated and look a lot like intricate clock mechanisms.

Look for red ("oil me here") dots, moving parts (turn the handwheel toward you a bit), plastic parts, and belts. The red dots identify points of high friction. If they are dry, put one drop of good-quality sewing-

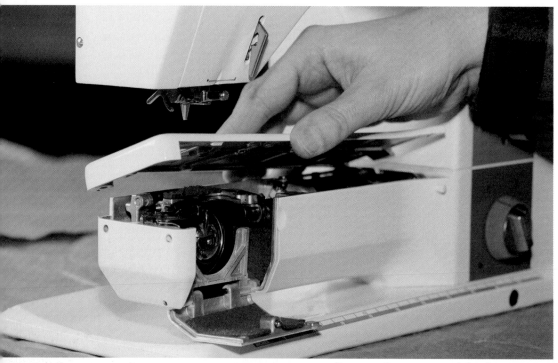

On most free-arm models, the top comes off so you can get inside. This one snaps in place, but most require you to loosen a screw or two. Use a cotton swab to clean the lint, threads, and grit from this area from time to time.

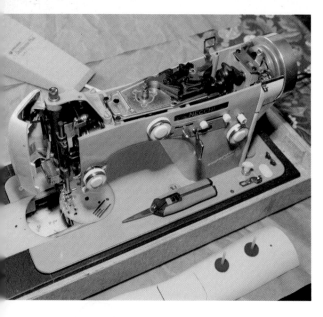

On most mechanical machines, the top comes off and the left end of the machine opens to reveal the light bulb and needle area. All machines have some kind of door that allows you to change the bobbin. This one slides to the left.

machine oil on each (see the photo at right). If your machine does not have any oiling dots, put a drop of oil on any point where two pieces of metal are moving against each other (plastic and nylon parts don't need oil). Are there any cracks in the plastic parts of your machine (hairline cracks may not matter right now, but keep your eye on them)? Are the drive belts worn thin, slipping, or cracked? If so, bring the machine to a reputable dealer and have those parts replaced before they cause serious damage. Turn the handwheel toward you. Things should be moving smoothly.

Now look at the left end of the machine. Unscrew the lightbulb and clean it with a nonabrasive household spray cleaner; it usually gets covered with fabric resins and oil film. Dry it well, but don't replace it yet. Clean the inside of the front cover to help diffuse more light onto your sewing. If the surface next to the lightbulb is dark or dull, you can improve the lighting by pasting a piece of aluminum foil there, shiny side out. If the bulb is very old, get a new one; it will be brighter. Your eyes are worth 59 cents.

Locate the upper part of the shaft that holds the needle. This is a high-friction area, so clean and oil this

Some manufacturers mark the oiling spots with red paint. If you keep your machine clean and sew only occasionally, one drop of oil in each of these spots every month or two should suffice. If you use your machine constantly, you might do light cleaning and oiling at the beginning of each day.

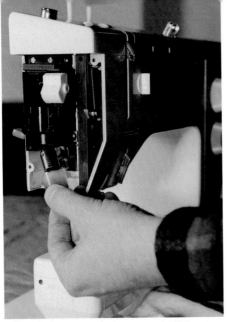

Make sure the light has been off for a while before removing the bulb—sewing-machine bulbs get very hot.

Once a year you should clean the area above the needle and under the top cover of the machine with a soft cloth or cotton swab. Lightly reoil the moving parts if your machine requires it.

shaft often. If you see a lot of fuzz, use a vacuum to suck it out. Most vacuums are too strong for this, so I just cover the mouth of my Dustbuster with duct tape, pierce a hole in the tape with a sharp pencil, and insert a plastic drinking straw (see the top photo on the facing page). It works great. Don't blow your own air or canned air into the machine; that just sends the dust deeper and will cause more problems later.

Does the needle shaft feel dry? If so, put a drop of oil on your finger and rub it up and down that part. Turn the handwheel toward you a few rotations to spread the oil around. Also put one drop of oil on the thread-uptake lever and the foot-pressure lever. Too much oil anywhere in this area of the machine will drip on your fabric, so use a light hand.

Replace the bulb. Put the lid and side panel back in place, and move on to the next step.

Cleaning the middle level of the machine

Accumulation of fibers, dust, grit, oil, and dead skin forms a "felt" under the feed dogs of all sewing machines. Eventually, this felt will prevent the dogs from rising to their proper height to pull back the fabric to make the stitch. Soon the stitches seem to get shorter in spite of the fact you haven't changed the stitch-length setting. When this felt really builds up and petrifies with age, the machine will stop feeding your fabric altogether.

Unscrew the plate below the needle (some just flip off; check your manual) to expose the feed dog and the area around it. Use a soft brush, a vacuum, and then a soft, cloth-covered cotton swab to clean out all the dirt, lint, and dust.

The bobbin area is another point of high friction on a sewing machine. Take out the removable parts and clean them regularly, following the directions in your manual (see the bottom photo at right). On some machines, the bobbin race is held in place by a clamp, but in others it is built in, and there is no case for the bobbin. No matter which kind, vacuum the dust, threads, and grit out now. If there is a heavy buildup, loosen the fuzz or felt with a brush with one hand while holding the vacuum near it with the other. After vacuuming, clean the part with a soft cloth or cotton swab on which you've put a drop of oil (see the top photo on p. 42). Again, don't blow the dust farther into the machine; the object is to get the dirt out, not to hide it!

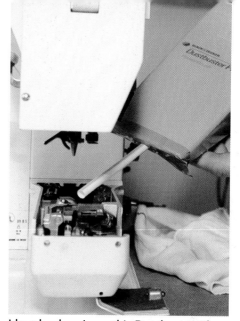

I laugh when I use this Dustbuster Plus because, for me, the plus is the tape and drinking straw. When cleaning, suck the dirt out with a vacuum. Don't blow it in farther with canned air.

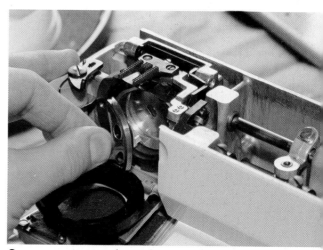

On any sewing machine, the place you have to clean the most is the bobbin area. If you sew a lot, take out the bobbin pieces and clean them every day. You'll hear the difference.

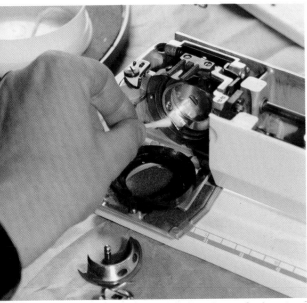

A cotton swab with a drop of oil on it will help you to remove lint and grit from the bobbin area.

Not all machines have a removable hook or a hook that needs oiling. Check your manual to see what maintenance is required for your machine. I've cleaned this hook with a soft cloth and am applying one tiny drop of oil on each side.

Never use a metal tool to clean around the bobbin area. Nicks and scratches on the hook destroy thread. If the nick or scratch is minor, you can probably smooth it out with a bit of crocus cloth from your hardware store. If the damage is serious, get a new race from your dealer. You don't have to bring in the machine, just the part.

Look at the hook carefully. There is an oil groove ⅛ in. from the edge on each side. Using your fingernail wrapped in a soft cloth, wipe out the groove. Now put one small drop of oil on each side of the hook (see the bottom photo) and fit it back into the shuttle (don't force it; it will fit right in if you turn it right). Lock the race into place, and close the bobbin area door. You're almost done. There's one more step—and it is an easy one.

Cleaning the lower level of the machine

Flatbed machines, especially those in tables or carrying cases, usually have no bottom cover (Singer machines are an exception; just remove the screws that are usually hidden in the rubber feet). Tilt the machine back on its hinges, and oil the moving parts just as you did on the top of the machine (see the

An oiler with a long, skinny neck makes it easy to place just a drop of oil on moving parts.

photo above). I like to tilt my machine back onto an old bed pillow, as this steadies it and makes it easier to work on (see the photo on p. 44).

Free-arm machines hide the lower mechanism of the machine under a small sleeve. Sometimes you get to these parts from the top of the free arm (on Bernina and Elna models, for example) and sometimes from the bottom. Some machines have a release lever, while others have screws. Check the manual to see if there are lubrication points on the bottom of your machine.

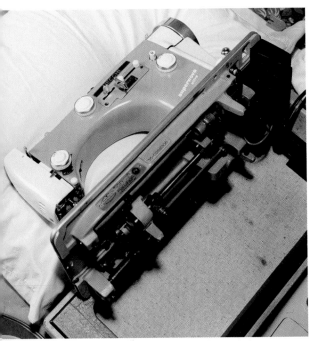

Older flatbed machines reveal their underworld workings when you tilt the machine out of the carrying case or the sewing table. This part of the machine must be cleaned and oiled every so often.

There, you're done. Set the machine right side up. Insert a new needle, and thread the machine with high-quality cotton. Put some fabric under the foot, plug her in, and step on the gas. Can you hear the difference?

Questions? Call a dealer that sells your brand of machine and ask. Good dealers don't mind answering maintenance questions, knowing that you will eventually bring the machine in for a major checkup or repair. But don't let the dealer talk you into a $40 tune-up if you can do it yourself.

HOW TO MODERNIZE AN OLD MACHINE

While an older sewing machine will never have the built-in conveniences of a computerized machine, there may be lots of reasons for you not to trade it in or throw it out. You may even consider buying a good used machine if the price and features suit you.

Older machines were built to last; that's why so many of them, perhaps yours, are still going strong. Because they have no electronic components, they are not affected by irregularities in electricity, and you need not fear using magnets like pin holders or seam guides around them. These quiet, smooth-running machines are relatively easy to keep in excellent working order; repairing them is usually inexpensive and uncomplicated assuming they have been taken care of over the years.

But the best reason for keeping your old machine may be the quality of the stitch. Some of these oldies produce the finest straight stitch you have ever seen; you need only to talk to the owner of a little Singer Featherweight to know what I'm talking about. That's all this Singer does, but it does it very, very well.

Another reason to keep your machine is that many hold on to a good portion of their value, and some are even worth more today than what they sold for originally. A used Bernina 830 or 930 is not cheap if you are lucky enough to find one. Sewers in the know wait in line for a used Pfaff 1222.

If money doesn't speak to you, then perhaps sentiment will. One of the best reasons to hold on to that old machine is that you love it. Perhaps it was given to you as a wedding present. Perhaps it was your mother's or grandmother's.

Perhaps you had to scrimp and save nickels and pennies to get it, or perhaps you used it to sew your first baby's clothes. You can't give up those memories, and you just can't give up that beautiful old machine. So don't.

With a few tricks I've learned over the years, you can modernize that older machine and feel like you've just gone out and spent a fortune on the latest top-of-the-line model. Well, almost!

Here are 10 ways to modernize an older machine.

Bobbin-empty indicator

New machines often beep or flash when the bobbin thread is about to run out. What a convenience, especially when you are doing decorative work. You can have this feature on an older machine by using this little trick: Before you start sewing, fill two bobbins with the same thread. Put one of them in the usual place, and use the other as the top thread. Since you use nearly the same amount of top and bottom thread, when the top bobbin is getting low, so is the one under the needle that you can't see. Voilà! A bobbin-empty indicator.

Needle up/down

Most new machines allow you to choose whether you want the needle to be in or out of the fabric when you stop sewing. You push a button, for example, and the needle always stops in the fabric—a very handy feature. By keeping your older machine in tip-top running order, by oiling it regularly, and by making sure the belts and foot control are in good shape, you can regulate the position of the needle with a simple tap of the control. A clean, well-oiled machine should be very sensitive to the foot control and not start and stop unpredictably. Have your machine tuned by your dealer or follow my cleaning and maintenance directions and you will be amazed at how responsive your machine can be.

Portability

Unlike older machines, most modern ones have built-in handles so you can carry them around. If your older machine is fixed into a sewing table, you can remove it and put it into a travel case. Ask your dealer if he has a good used case that fits your machine. Because your older machine is probably heavy, you can then put it on a luggage carrier and wheel it around. You can remove a flatbed (as opposed to a free-arm) machine from its carrying case or table and set it on any tabletop or flat surface. It has built-in metal feet that allow it to stand upright for repairs. Make a heavy-duty canvas carrier much like one used to carry logs, and you have turned your stationary machine into a portable.

Quiet function

Many of the older machines are actually quieter than newer ones. But you can soften the sound of any machine by putting it on a carpet square or a rubberized place mat (see the photo on the facing page). This will reduce vibration and keep the machine from sliding around. If your machine is in a sewing table, you can quiet it considerably by putting some flannel or sound-deadening foam in the space underneath it.

Horizontal thread feed

When thread is unwinding from a vertical spool, it tugs at the spool itself, causing drag and friction. Modern machines and some older ones, such as the Singer Touch and Sew models, allow you to place the spools horizontally so the thread slips off without turning the spool. The result is a smoother stitch. You can have this feature for a few dollars by buying a thread stand. A thread stand allows the spool to remain stationary, while the thread is brought up vertically and then carried over to the machine. The heavy metal stands are the best, but you can use the cheaper plastic version by putting some modeling clay in the cavity underneath so the stand won't tip when you use a large cone of thread.

Fancy stitches

One of the most seductive qualities of newer machines is their astonishing menu of stitches that you can call up, often at the push of a button. You will never get these stitches on your 1939 Singer, but chances are you have one of those Sears, Elna, or Brother models that came with cams—the little, round plastic things that you never use. Dust them off and use them. There are probably other types of cams besides the ones that came with your machine, so ask your dealer if he has them. A box of cams should cost only a few dollars. Some of these cams (Elna, for example) are marked so that you know where the pattern begins and ends. If yours have no marks, it's easy to mark them. Cut out a small triangle from the sticky portion of a Post-it note and put it on the cam where the pattern

All machines benefit from sitting on a piece of carpeting, which is what you'll see them on in any dealership, or on a rubberized place mat. Either one will lessen vibration and noise and will also keep your seam ripper from rolling around.

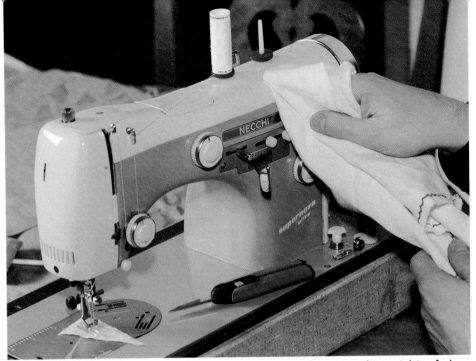

An old, soft T-shirt is perfect for cleaning the surface of your machine. A bit of glass cleaner should remove light soil; add a dot of toothpaste to remove stains or scratches from plastic.

begins. Put a similar mark on the machine opposite the cam. When the two triangles meet, you'll know you are at the end of the pattern.

Good lighting

Older machines (and many modern ones for that matter) often have very poor lighting in the needle area. Modern machines use quartz lights that provide a whiter, brighter light. But you can have excellent lighting by simply taking out and cleaning or replacing the bulb. Most of the bulbs in older machines last a long time but yellow with age. You can also line the inside of the light area with a small piece of aluminum foil, shiny side out. Use a glue stick to set it in place. Of course, the best way to improve lighting on any machine is to do what's done in commercial sewing—buy a cheap gooseneck lamp and set it so you can direct the light just where you want it. If you don't like the idea of setting the lamp on your sewing table, buy a cheap 1950s gooseneck floor lamp, put it at your right elbow, and aim one of the lights at the needle area.

Automatic needle threader

It's such a great idea, but how many built-in needle threaders have you seen that actually work? Not many are useful. But there is a very simple thing you can do to "automatically" thread any machine; my Aunt Jane taught it to me ages ago, and I'm passing this professional "secret" on to you. Never unthread your machine. When you want to change the top thread, cut it off at the spool. Tie the new thread to the old with a box knot and, with the presser foot level in its up position, pull the knot through the entire system until it gets to the eye of the needle. At that point, hold the thread on both sides of the needle and gently pull the knot through. You just automatically threaded your machine in a few seconds.

Auto thread holder/cutter

Almost all new machines have a little clip and blade just above and to the left of the needle area to hold and cut your thread. Some older machines have a piece of black steel clipped to the foot shank, but I never liked these very much. Here are two things you can do: First, for $3 you can buy a holder/cutter and paste it to the side of your machine.

Or if you are a do-it-yourselfer, you can simply tape a bent, smooth paper clip to the bed of your machine. The clip will hold the thread, but it won't cut it.

Shiny new exterior

Let's face it—a new machine is a new machine. Just like a new car, it smells good, looks good, and feels good. When was the last time you took your machine to the beauty parlor? Get some cotton swabs, a soft cloth, household spray cleaner, and machine oil. Loosen screws and get into those corners with that grease-and-oil remover. Dry the machine well with the cloth, then put a drop of machine oil (but never 3-in-One oil) on that cloth and polish it up. Go ahead, dab a little of your favorite perfume on that soft cloth and rub it over the machine to make her smell pretty. You know that a clean car drives better; well, a clean machine sews better, too.

CHAPTER FOUR

Smart Ways to Buy a Sewing Machine

Since I recommend buying the best sewing machine you can afford, the kind of machine you consider should be determined by your budget. For example, if you have only $500 to spend, your choices are to buy a once top-of-the-line used machine or buy a new, cheaply made model. I recommend buying the used machine. If you can afford to spend more than $1,000, I recommend looking at some of the new computerized models.

Whether you shop for a new or used sewing machine, you should ask yourself what you liked and disliked about your old one (see the checklist on the facing page) and what features you require of any sewing machine, new or used.

CONSIDERING A USED MACHINE

We all have our limits when it comes to buying used stuff; I know some people who would rather die

before they would buy anything used. Never mind that their homes are filled with items acquired in antique shops and auctions. I suppose those items were not used—they were just cherished!

I was surprised by one of my own prejudices not long ago when I was "junking" with my friend Julie Ann. I offhandedly said to her that I would never buy a used mattress and didn't understand the mentality of anyone who would. She gently reminded me that, ex-Peace Corps, international businessperson that I was, I had probably slept on some of the most "interesting" mattresses in the world. "And who," she said, "do you think slept on those mattresses before you arrived at the hotel?" Good point, Julie Ann!

The cleanliness factor is not the only reason why people avoid used appliances. When you are paying hundreds of dollars for a used item, you want to know that you aren't wasting your money. You want to

What Do You Like and Dislike about Your Current Machine?

Bring a checklist of what you like and dislike about your old machine when you go shopping for another one.

Likes

❏ Nobody is going to steal it
❏ Easy to use
❏ Basic stitches
❏ Good stitch quality
❏ Flatbed machine
❏ Easy to clean and repair
❏ Smooth running
❏ Reliable
❏ Sews speedily
❏ Sentimental value
❏ Looks old, very sexy
❏ Other _____

Dislikes

❏ Limited functions
❏ Slow speed
❏ Few stitches
❏ Poor wiring, motor
❏ Poor stitch quality
❏ Heavy to carry around
❏ Bad lighting
❏ Tension is always off
❏ Noisy
❏ Costly to repair
❏ Difficult to thread
❏ Looks old, not sexy
❏ Other _____

know if you can you return the item if it doesn't work properly and if there is a guarantee.

Here are some good reasons to consider buying a used sewing machine.

- Most used machines are models that are no longer in production. But not all used machines are old or discontinued. In fact, many people trade in near brand-new machines because they have to have the latest technology or the latest status symbol. Many sewers keep their older, reliable machine and buy a used second machine.

- Used machines cost less than new ones of the same quality. If you are not a maniac for the latest have-it-or-die model, take advantage of another's disposable consumerism to pick up a good buy. Last year Jill might have spent $2,000 for her machine and this year she is selling it for $1,000. Not a bad discount for a one-year-old machine that has been well taken care of.

- Some older sewing machines make better stitches and run more smoothly than some new models. Just because a machine is older doesn't mean it isn't good, especially if it was once top of the line.

- You help to recycle. Give that machine a home and help to keep something out of the junkyard.
- If the machine is a classic, once top-of-the-line model in good condition, it will retain a lot of its value. You can always sell it and recoup most of your money.

Having said all that, my mother is sometimes right: Buying something used can mean buying someone else's problems. So when buying anything—new or used—you do better if you know what you want, do your homework, and take some sensible precautions. The chart on the facing page lists some places to look for used machines and the level of risk you take when you buy.

Oldies with goodies

Generally speaking, older machines cannot offer you all the conveniences of a computerized modern machine, but some older machines still rival the new ones for their quality. Here are some respected manufacturers and which of their brands I recommend.

Baby Lock This company made a name for itself in the serger industry, and it now mostly sells machines made by Brother. I haven't seen many of these machines on the used-machine market, perhaps because they are new and good.

Bernina Any Swiss-made Bernina (especially models 830, 910, 930, and 1230) is a treasure worth keeping, and that is why they are difficult to find on the secondhand market. If you happen to find one for sale and it meets your sewing needs, snap it up. Quilters go bonkers for these machines.

Brother This company has always made exceptional, high-end machines and unexceptional, cheaper chain-store models, which I don't recommend. If you can find one of the more expensive models, it is worth a look. These machines will last almost forever.

Elna Recent Elna machines have been made by Japanese companies, but some of the older, Swiss-made models from the 1970s were very innovative and are collector's items. Look for the much-loved Elna Super, Lotus, or Carina, and some of the smaller, lightweight gems.

Where to Find Used Machines

Where to find it	Risk level
Garage sale or secondhand store	Very risky. Only for old fix-it-up guys and gals.
Friend	Could be a good buy, especially if you know the history of the machine. If you are not sure of the machine's condition, suggest that the sale include a trip to a reliable dealer for a mechanical checkup before you buy. Doing so will preserve your friendship in the long run.
Antique shop	I thought you wanted to sew?
Want ads	Great possibilities here, but be careful. This is a great way to buy a very current model. The seller might have made a mistake and cannot return it to the dealer. Test the machine before you buy. Once you hand over the money, the money is his and the machine is yours. Call dealerships to find out current prices of the model for sale.
Sewing-machine dealer	Your most reliable source for a used machine. Test before you buy (some dealers will let you take the machine home for the weekend). Insist on a one-year parts and labor guarantee on an older machine or a two-year guarantee on a newer one, even if you have to pay a little extra for it.

Kenmore Sears machines have always been manufactured by various companies (mostly Japanese today) to Sears' specifications. Generally speaking, Sears has always sold reliable, basic machines for the average American sewer. You can call the Sears repair department and ask if the company still stocks the parts for the model you are considering.

New Home (Janome) Like Brother, this Japanese company produces high-end and low-end machines. The older, more expensive models were usually well made and innovative, while the low-end models were designed for chain stores. Again, I don't recommend the low-end models.

Necchi This Italian manufacturer now produces mostly low-end models in the Far East, but it was once a leader in innovation in the sewing industry. Any Necchi machine made before 1980 is worth a look, especially one in the Supernova series (1957) and the unusual-looking but superb-sewing computerized Suprema IV.

Pfaff All older metal Pfaffs were built like tanks, and people wait on line for some of them, especially a model 1222 or any other model with a walking foot. Newer electronic models that have needle up/down options and bobbin-empty indicators are especially nice machines.

Singer From time to time, people go crazy over a Singer model; these days little, black (sometimes white) Singer Featherweights are selling for astronomical prices. Other models have also been innovative and reliable workhorses, like the Touch and Sew series of the 1950s and 1960s. Avoid Singer's early computerized models.

Viking Most older Viking machines were well built and innovative. Some of their recent electronic (as opposed to computerized) models are worth a look (especially the 1100). Many Viking owners traded the excellent #1 for the #1+, which adds embroidery. If you can find the #1 at a good price, snap it up.

White Now owned by Viking, the White Sewing Machine Company made some good middle-price-range machines. Check with a Viking dealer to find out if parts are available.

Parts for Used Machines

Sewing-machine manufacturers are required to keep an inventory of parts for out-of-production machines for as long as the warranty sold with the machine (usually 15 to 20 years). The cost of keeping these parts is expensive, so the parts don't come cheaply to the dealer or to you. Local dealers themselves also keep old trade-in machines and cannibalize them for parts. If you have a machine that you love dearly and don't want to see it bite the dust, buy its healthy twin for a few bucks at a garage sale. Then you'll have spare parts to replace yourself or to bring to the dealer when you need them.

What to do with your old machine

If you have decided that you want another—new or used—machine, here are your options as to what to do with your old machine:

- Keep the old machine and buy another because you intend to use both. If you have the space and the old machine has some redeeming qualities that you really enjoy and can still use, keep it. If, after a few weeks or months, you find that you will never take the old one out of the closet and use it, sell it or give it away.
- Give the old one to Goodwill and buy another machine. If your old machine is ready for the junkyard, give it to the junk man. But if it works, think about passing it on to someone who doesn't mind using a basic machine. Give it to Goodwill, a college student on a tight budget, or a kid who wants to learn how to sew. But don't give a machine that is dysfunctional to anyone. That will only frustrate the recipient and may put her off sewing forever.

  If your machine has naught but sentimental value for you, think about taking a picture of it and keeping that on your bulletin board. Or transfer the good karma by pasting the picture of your old "friend" onto your next machine. Then give the old machine to a charity where you know it will get good use. You will be doubly blessed!
- Trade the old one in for a new machine. To get your business, most dealers will give you something for an old machine even if it is useless to them. I

know one dealer that will give you a dollar a pound for your old machine; he doesn't give up much since the heaviest clunkers weigh in at 40 pounds.

- Sell your old machine on the open market. If your machine is in good working order, you may get more money by selling it yourself than by trading it in to a dealer. A dealer might suggest how much you should ask for it, or you could check the blue book price (see the sidebar on p. 76).

If your machine is worth less than $100, try word-of-mouth advertising, bulletin boards in the supermarket, and Internet ads. If your machine is worth more, you may want to put an ad in your local Sunday paper, which will cost you between $20 and $40. Don't forget to subtract the cost of the ad and your time from the selling price. Clean and oil the machine, and present it in a good atmosphere when a buyer comes to call. Smile, look nice—you have just become a sewing-machine dealer!

CHOOSING A NEW MACHINE

After considering a used machine, you may decide after all that you want to buy a new one. I'll tell you how you should choose one, including some features you may want to look for on a new machine. I'll also give you some tips on how you should test a machine before buying. But first, if you're like me, you take sewing machines for granted and don't spend much time thinking about how they are made. Recently, I was fortunate enough to learn firsthand about the process of bringing a sewing machine from the drawing board to the market.

My trip to a sewing-machine factory

I had the privilege of visiting the home office and factory of one of the world's premier sewing-machine companies: Fritz Gegauf, Ltd., the manufacturer of Bernina machines. I spent three days in northeastern Switzerland with significant members of the company talking about the future of sewing, marketing products, design of future machines, and sewing education. I was sworn to secrecy on a lot of exciting things I saw and heard, but I can tell you this: a heck of a lot of hard work goes into making a sewing machine.

You can't imagine how much time and effort Bernina team members spend thinking, planning, designing, engineering, manufacturing, assembling, and marketing their products. The sewing educators, engineers, and marketers, all with the help of input from dealers and consumers, plan years ahead to bring a new model to the market. Not only do they have to predict the future needs of sewers but they also have to take into account sewing trends (will quilting continue to be strong in the year 2000?), the aging population (will baby boomers need larger displays and buttons as their eyesight weakens?), and cultural differences (sewers in Europe, for example, do not sew the same things or for the same reasons as sewers in the United States).

At Bernina (and throughout the industry, I'm sure), the talk around the conference table came to the same points over and over again: How can we make an affordable sewing machine and keep the quality high? How can we bring sewing back into the schools? What will the sewing trends of tomorrow be?

New technology is forever being tested to improve the sewing machine. New plastics are as tough or tougher than metal but weigh much less, which is important when producing a portable machine. Several tiny step motors replace the single motor of older models. When the consumers want a special foot for sewing quilts, the Bernina engineers go to work designing one. It takes months before the foot is available from your dealer.

Sewing-machine manufacturing is a risky business. If the company makes a false move by introducing a bad product, it could be ruined. If the company makes one kind of machine and the consumer wants another, it has missed the boat and winds up with a warehouse full of machines nobody wants.

During my visit to the Bernina offices, the Bernina machine for the year 2000 was off the drawing boards and stood before us as a series of five nonworking shells. The owner of the company asked: Which one looks like a Bernina but not so much like the other models that it doesn't have a personality of its own? Which shape will make sewing more comfortable? Which shape will be attractive to new sewers? What colors will be hot three years from now?

Next to the dummy models were the "guts" of the machine—the mechanical innards. The head engineer explained how it works. Others asked: Can we have this? Can we have that? The answer is always the same: Sure. I can give you anything you want, but it will raise the cost of the machine. What will the consumer pay for?

The sewing instructors looked at the buttons on the working model and asked the engineers when was the last time they actually sewed anything. What were they thinking when they put that button there? Engineer logic versus sewer logic. Like in any good partnership, the negotiating began. I can give up this, but not that. We can keep this if we use this kind of new money-saving technology. We can keep this by making it an option.

Meanwhile, in the factory, dozens of workers were making parts of machines that had been approved

Different Name, Same Machine

If you look in *Consumer Reports* for information on washing machines, you will see more than a dozen brands on the charts. Names like Amana, Kenmore, General Electric, and Speed Queen are familiar. But if you read the text, you will find that many of those names are made by the same company. General Electric also makes Hot Point, while Amana makes Speed Queen. And since Sears doesn't make its own appliances, their Kenmore models are made by somebody else. It's a fact of consumer life today.

The same thing is true of sewing machines. There are many labels on the market but the number of manufacturers is shrinking. Necchi, an Italian company, used to make high-quality sewing machines in Italy. Now their mostly low-end machines are made by a company in Japan.

Now American owned, Elna used to make its machines in Switzerland. High-end Elna machines are made by the Janome Company of Japan, which also makes the New Home line and machines for Sears. Pfaff of Germany was bought by Singer of Hong Kong and they are beginning to "exchange" products.

What this means to you is that you will find fewer and fewer interesting differences between machines since the technology is shared by more than one brand. And it means that you can shop for price. If two products are exactly the same except for the name and price, which one would you buy?

for production. Employees oversaw giant vats of pink stones that vibrate for hours to polish delicate metal parts to a mirror finish. Holes were drilled. Electronic boards had to be tested. The famous Bernina feet were assembled and adjusted one by one to ensure sewing accuracy. The parts reached the assembly teams: six people worked together to assemble an entire machine. The first person had nothing but parts in front of her; the last person was testing the stitches on the completely assembled machine.

And so it went, through packing, shipping, and delivery until the machine appeared in your dealer's showroom, then on your sewing table.

How to choose a sewing machine the right way

While it is sometimes fun to fling caution to the wind and buy on impulse, for most of us buying a car

A Mini-Lesson in Sewing-Machine Economics

You have to look closely at the product literature and on the metal label on the back, side, or bottom of a sewing machine these days to find out where it was made.

Some machines that boldly and proudly proclaim *engineered* in country X (usually in Europe) are actually *manufactured* in Asia. There is a good business reason for this: It's less costly to make a machine in Taiwan where the average hourly wage is much less than in the United States or Europe. But the manufacturer knows that its customers want to buy a machine made in a country noted for its fine watches (Switzerland), fast trains (Germany), beautiful steel knives (Sweden), or all of the above (Japan). So to keep competitive, these companies try to have the best of both worlds: They design the machine at home, then have it made less expensively where labor costs are lower. Many Japanese machines are now manufactured in China, Korea, Taiwan, or Thailand.

The bottom line is a good company will stand behind its products no matter where the products are manufactured. A company that sells shoddy merchandise in a competitive market soon loses customer loyalty, market share, and your business.

or any major appliance, including a sewing machine, is not something to be done on a whim. After all, you are going to have to live with your purchase for a long time. And yet, most people make buying decisions the wrong way.

Let me give you an example that involves buying a computer: People often decide whether or not they want an IBM or a Macintosh, buy one, choose the software that will run on that machine, then go home and use it.

The reverse should happen. First, you should decide what you want to do with the computer (word processing, keep a large file of data you can look up easily, do your taxes), then you should find and buy the software that does the tasks you want to do and the way you like to do them. Once you have the software you like, ask the clerk what machines the software runs on. Then you buy the best machine you can afford that runs that software, no matter what the brand.

Buying a sewing machine is not any different. You shouldn't start by asking what brand you should buy. You should start by asking yourself what you want to sew.

Last year, I wrote an article for *Threads* magazine that challenged sewing-machine manufacturers to pool their machines' great features so we could have one machine that "does it all." One year later, we are no closer to the machine that "does it all" than before. Each brand continues to offer something that the others don't; it is still up to you, the consumer, to find the machine that fits your sewing preferences and your sewing temperament.

Nonetheless, there may be a sewing machine that makes you very happy even with some short-comings. And if you have the money and the space, a second machine might be useful where your primary machine isn't. For example, maybe your primary machine is wonderful but too heavy to transport to class. A smaller, more portable model might be just the thing to take along at times like these. You might be missing some of the bells and whistles that are on the big machine, but you can't sew on the best of machines with a bad back either!

Hardware features

Here are some hardware features you might look for when shopping for a new machine.

Good lighting Poor lighting can make sewing difficult, and uneven lighting can give you a headache. Look for a machine that has more than one light source, with one to the left and one to the right of the needle.

Speed control Many sewing tasks need reduced speed for good control and accuracy. Insist on at least two speeds; a fast-to-slow sliding speed button is better.

Instant reverse On old machines, this button or lever is always on the far right, but it is better placed directly above the needle. The larger the button is the better, so you can just raise your finger and touch it while you sew.

Sewing surface Most machines now come with slide-on accessory boxes that serve as mini-sewing tables. They are inadequate at best, so look for a machine that comes with an attachable, larger sewing surface. For accurate sewing, a larger surface is a must.

Foot-pressure control The foot pushes the fabric down on the feed "teeth" to move it forward, backward, and sideways. Different fabrics need different pressures, but on many machines this isn't adjustable. If you want to sew delicate or heavy fabrics, look for this feature.

Feed dogs These are the teeth that move the fabric for sewing. Most are good, but they can be closer or further apart depending on the width of the zigzag stitch on the machine. It is easier to turn fabric when the teeth are closer together, so if you sew a lot of intricate things, you may want close teeth like they are on many older machines with a 4mm stitch.

Walking foot Feed dogs pull the bottom layer of fabric, but what pulls the top layer through? Nothing, and this causes the bottom to feed a little faster than the top, making it difficult to keep the ends matched. A top-feeding system can help. Built in or as an attachment, this feature is handy, especially for sewing slippery fabrics or plaids.

Sewing foot The right foot helps you place stitches accurately. If the foot wobbles or isn't made well, it will not guide the fabric into the needle accurately, and you will not be happy. Also, a good foot is well marked and easy to look at for long periods of time; the less shiny it is the better.

Needle threader There are all kinds of needle-threading systems, but only some of them work well. If threading the needle is a problem for you, ask the dealer to let you use the needle-threading contraption that comes with the machine. And try it yourself; don't just watch the dealer do it.

Automatic thread cutter Some machines automatically cut the upper and lower (bobbin) threads at the push of a button when you are finished sewing. This is a handy feature, especially on machines that do embroidery. Otherwise, most machines have a small holder/cutter on the left side of the machine.

Bobbins Bobbins have to be small for technical reasons, but some are so dinky you have to fill them too often. The larger the bobbin the better.

Bobbin-empty indicator A machine with this feature will tell you when the bobbin thread is running low. Some machines blink and some beep. I like the beep unless the blink is a little red light that I will notice.

Hook The hook carries the top thread around the bobbin to make stitches. A well-designed hook will make beautiful stitches and won't jam. To test this feature, sew the beginning of a seam without holding the ends of the threads for the first few stitches. If the machine sews the first few stitches without jamming, you have a jam-free hook.

Foot lifter Just when the project is placed perfectly under the needle, you have to let go to lower the foot lever, which is placed behind the machine. Of course, everything slips and you have to start over again. With a slight movement of your knee, a foot lifter raises and lowers the foot so you don't have to let go of the fabric. It's really a blessing.

Automatic tension Some stitches require different thread tensions, and on most machines you have to remember to change the setting when you go from one stitch to another. Newer machines have tension that changes automatically when you select the stitch. It's a very desirable feature.

Pedal The pedal starts and stops the machine and controls the speed. Poorly built ones are lightweight, slide around, and make the machine sew in fits and spurts. Look for one that is heavy enough to stay put, large enough to hold your entire foot, and sensitive enough to let you sew with precision.

Bobbin winder Bobbins need to be wound evenly and at moderate speed so the thread doesn't stretch. Newer machines have a separate motor for the bobbin winder, so you don't have to dink with the handwheel on the right side of the machine. Some machines allow you to fill the bobbin with thread right from the needle, a handy feature.

Stitches and functions

Here are some stitches and functions you might look for when shopping for a new machine.

Stitch variety Computerized models offer the most stitches, with some machines having open systems that let you add stitches via purchased cassette, computer linkup, or built-in stitch designer. If you intend to do only basic sewing, a good mechanical machine with a handful of stitches should do.

Horizontal and vertical pattern flip You can double the stitch effects by flipping the stitches over to create new combinations and new utilities. For example, you can flip a blanket stitch over and keep your bulky blanket on the left side of the needle as you sew. Most computerized machines have horizontal flip; the better ones have vertical flip as well.

Pattern begin, count, half, and end Computerized sewing allows you to automatically start a pattern at its beginning, then sew the pattern as a half, a whole, or in multiples. If you like decorating your projects with letters, numbers, and decorative stitches, you will appreciate these functions.

Double-needle function If you like to sew with a double needle, you must remember to limit the zigzag width of your stitches or you will break the needle. Computerized machines will automatically limit the stitch width for you.

Temporary memory and stitch recorder When you make changes to a stitch—say you set the length at 2.5mm instead of 2.0mm—you don't want to have to repeat the change each time you return to that stitch after you have used another. Ask the dealer if the machine you are considering will remember the setting you have chosen, including the needle position, speed, and other function choices.

Some machines can record stitches as you sew them. Touch a button to start the recording and touch it again to stop. Now the machine "plays back" the stitches as many times as you wish. This is very handy if you are sewing the same thing over and over again, such as when assembling a patchwork.

Permanent memory If you like to sew names or complicated assemblages of decorative stitches or like a special setting for a buttonhole, it is important that you have a place to save your recipe. If this function appeals to you, look for a machine that has plenty of memory "mailboxes" and plenty of room in each mailbox to store your creation. Ask the dealer what the memory capacity of the machine is.

Tacking, fixing, and knotting If you don't somehow knot the threads at the end of your sewing, they will, of course, come undone in a matter of time. Back tacking isn't always possible on decorative work, so you want the machine to automatically make a few stitches in place to lock the threads. If you do a lot of decorative sewing, this feature is a must.

On-screen help Since machines are getting so smart, they can memorize the operations manual and give you help instantly when you ask for it. If you are a beginning sewer, you might appreciate this feature that advanced sewers might never use.

Buttonholes Nothing makes a garment look more amateurish than poorly sewn buttonholes. Top-of-the-line computerized models will give you lots of styles of buttonholes and can repeat them to your specifications automatically. Different companies use different methods to achieve this. You'll have to try the machines out to find the one that you like.

Needle positions—up/down, right/left For some sewing, you always want the needle to stop in the fabric so you can turn or adjust the fabric without it slipping. The needle up/down button on many machines will allow you to choose how the needle stops. Some machines allow you to change the needle position with a tap of the pedal. For accurate sewing, it is convenient to be able to locate the needle to the right or left of center. Basic machines give you 3 position choices, while elaborate ones give you as many as 25. Ten sounds like more than enough to me.

Eleven things to do to test any sewing machine

The only way to find the right machine for you is to try it out and

Large Stitches, Sideways Stitches, Embroidery Stitches

Early sewing machines sewed a simple straight stitch backward and forward, and sewers thought that was a miracle. Next came sideways needle movement that produced a 4mm-wide zigzag stitch. In combination with the forward motion, sideways needle movement could produce some simple patterns. Combined with forward *and* backward motion, it could produce some wonderful utility stitches.

Next, a wider zigzag up to 9mm allowed more complicated stitch designs. The stitch was restricted, but a 9mm scallop stitch is very impressive when you compare it to one less than half that size.

What would happen, the sewing-machine engineers asked, if we could move the fabric from side to side as well as forward and backward? They came up with sideways-motion machines, where the teeth under the fabric move the fabric in all directions, that go beyond the needle-motion limitation. Now you could sew stitches the size of a silver dollar.

What about a design larger than 40mm? Just put the fabric in a 5-in. by 7-in. or larger hoop, and let the machine automatically move the fabric all around. The needle doesn't have to do anything but go up and down to produce exquisite multicolored, hand-sized embroideries.

What could be next?

see if it fits. When you go shopping, here are some things you should do.

1. Take your time. If possible, call the dealer to make an appointment. It's your money and your decision, so don't rush.

2. Let the dealer or owner show you how to use the machine. He will show it off to its (and his) best advantage. When he is through with the demo, thank him and tell him politely and firmly to step aside. You are going to test the machine. If he balks at letting you try the machine, find another dealer.

3. Ask the dealer or owner to put the machine back in its case. You should start by unpacking the machine just as if you were taking it out of the box at home. Can you easily lift it? Does the handle feel sturdy? Is the machine easy to prepare for sewing?

4. Check the wires, especially on a used machine. They should be supple, not brittle and cracked.

Carefully check the machine's exterior. Are there any cracks or chips on the machine? If there are a lot of scratches around the needle-plate area, it's a good sign the machine was well used. If there are cracks or dents on the machine, it could have been dropped. Reject it.

5. Change the needle, even on a new machine. You are going to have to do that eventually, so you might as well know now if it is easy to do. Check under the needle plate. Is it easy to get to for cleaning out lint and threads? Is it clean down there? If it's dirty under there, the machine has been well used and the dealer has not prepared it for sale. He should clean it.

6. Run the unthreaded machine. Listen to the motor. Does it sound healthy? Do you hear grinding, clickety-clacks, or stressful humming before the machine begins to sew?

7. Fill a bobbin and install it. Install the upper thread. Is it easy or difficult?

8. Take out your fabric samples and sew a little project typical of what you normally sew. For example, sew a pocket on a larger piece of fabric. Make a buttonhole. Sew in reverse. Try something decorative. If the machine has a memory, use it. Spend at least 30 minutes playing with the machine.

9. Compare your checklist of things that you liked and didn't like about your old machine with the new machine. If you didn't like something on your old machine, why would you buy the same feature now? If there was some feature missing from your old machine, will you get it on this one?

10. Look at the manual. Is it going to be a good friend when you get the machine home? Is it clearly written? Are there plenty of photos that illustrate threading, setup, and, on computerized models, use of the information on the screens?

11. Take your "project" over to a window and really look at the stitching in good, natural light. Is it up to your standards? The stitching is never going to look better, so make sure you are satisfied.

HOW TO BUY THE MACHINE YOU LIKE

Make all the fancy decisions you want about this sewing-machine feature or that, but it gets to the

Things to Bring with You when You Test a Machine

The atmosphere in a sewing-machine store is designed to sell sewing machines, and the biggest part of the atmosphere is the seller herself. If the salesperson is skilled at sewing and selling, the machine she is using will seem like it does everything and does everything well. That's because she knows how to handle the quirks of the machine, and she knows what *not* to show you. You must sit at the machine yourself and take it for a spin. Here are some things you should take along:

- Fabric scraps from your last few sewing projects. If you are going to sew Polarfleece gloves on your machine, it isn't going to do you any good to have stiff cotton swatches (what dealers call demo cloth) to sew on.
- Your eyeglasses.
- The checklist of things you liked and disliked about your old machine. Did you forget how annoying that feature was now that it's in a shiny new box?
- The company brochure that lists all the exclusive features of the model you are looking at. Check them out one by one.
- A note pad or sticky notes to apply to the brochure of that model. Write down the model number, the suggested retail price, the selling price, and the things you liked and disliked about the machine. If you look at several machines, you'll forget what belonged to what.
- Your sewing shoes. Carry them in a bag if they can't be worn into the shop.

Here's what not to bring: your credit card, checkbook, or cash. You are testing the machine, not buying it. Put all your energy into seeing if this is the right machine for you, and don't worry about bargaining. There is no point in getting a good deal on a machine that you won't be happy with. On your next visit, which could be as soon as a few hours later (but I'd sleep on it), you will focus on getting the best deal you can.

point where there is nothing left to do but reach into your pocket and take out the money to pay for the decisions you've made. The chart on the facing page gives you an idea of the kind of machine you'll get for the money.

There is more than one way to pay for a sewing machine, and you should consider the advantages and disadvantages of all of them before you make your purchase. For example, if you can save some money by paying cash, perhaps you can afford that more expensive machine after all.

Ten ways to save for that machine

Well, if you're like me, you just hate to spend good money on things you know you can get for what seems like nothing. So here are 10 ways I use to get the things I want without dipping into the pockets of my retirement fund.

1. Save your small change in an opaque container (clear glass is too tempting) that you mark Sewing Machine Fund. Ask your husband to empty his pockets into your fund.
2. Recycle big time. Collect soft drink bottles and cans and put the money toward your machine. Get the kids to help

you, but be fair and give them a cut of the action.
3. Give sewing lessons to neighborhood children or teach an evening class for community education. If you are an accomplished sewer, you might teach for a sewing-machine dealer and get two advantages: some cash and a deep discount on that machine you want.
4. Give something up. This is an old "Lent" trick I was taught when I was in grade school: Give up that piece of candy and give the money to the poor. Well, give up that cappuccino and put that two bucks into the sewing machine fund. When you get your machine, sew something useful and pretty and donate it to charity.
5. Sell something you don't need. If I really want something badly and don't have the money, I make a sweep of the house and collect all the things I don't need or want. Then I have a garage sale or bring better clothes to a consignment shop.
6. Make or grow something to sell. Are you good at propagating houseplants? Sell them at your next neighborhood sale. Do you

Price Points for Household Sewing Machines

What you pay	What you get
$4,000+	A machine with all the capabilities of a $2,500 machine plus the ability to attach it to your home computer. The software that allows the two machines to understand each other is expensive.
$2,500+	A top-of-the-line sewing and embroidery machine. Can do sideways-motion sewing. Has every stitch you can imagine plus the ability to buy more on cards.
$1,500-$2,300	A top-of-the-line sewing machine only. Has maximum features and a generous menu of built-in stitches. *Or* an embroidery-only machine. *Or* a lower-quality combination embroidery and sewing machine but with no sideways-motion stitches.
$1,000	Popular price point. A good machine with all the basics. These are often anniversary or special-edition models.
$700	A machine with some interesting features but is made from cheaper materials and is designed to last half as long as the higher-priced models.
$250-$500	The "thrift" end of the line that is often made in another country and given a different name so as not to contaminate the reputation of the higher-priced models. Never buy anything called a "jeans" machine.
$150 or less	Variety-store junk.

A Short Story about Buying

My sewing room is in the basement of my house. It's cool and damp in summer (requiring a dehumidifier) and cold and dry in winter (requiring a humidifier and heater). Except for occasional clear, dry, and warm days (two days a year in my neck of the woods!), the windows stay shut.

An ad in the Sunday paper convinced me that an air purifier might take some of the dust and mold out of the air to make the sewing room more pleasant. This contraption used special new technology, and—music to my ears—it was on sale. I was ready to buy it.

I don't part with $200 easily, so there was one small question I had to ask before I went to the store: Did these things actually work? So I consulted a 1993 *Consumer Reports* digest and found a helpful two-page article on air purifiers, what they claim to do, and how well they perform the task. I got my answer and saved $200.

Learning about sewing machines may not be as fun as spending money, but you really do need to learn a bit before you choose one. There are many different brands and kinds of sewing machines, as well as different price points, so be sure to do some research before buying.

make good jams and jellies or homemade soaps? Sell them at the farmer's market.

7. Take a temporary sales job at Christmastime.

8. Comb the classified ads to find what you want and then barter. I'll give you this great canoe for your machine. You have nothing to lose, and the person just might say yes.

9. Write about sewing. Did you know that sewing magazines pay you to tell about your unusual sewing projects? They will even pay you for sewing tips they can pass on to their readers. Don't worry about your writing skills; the magazine editor will edit the story for you.

10. Sell your blood. Check with your doctor; you may have a gold mine running through those veins!

Kinds of sewing-machine dealerships

Once you've saved your pennies, it's time to go shopping. Not all sewing-machine dealerships are equal. Some carry only one brand, some two, and

The Gratz family has been operating a single-brand dealership and selling Vikings in the Twin Cities area for years. Recently, they added the New Home line. The machines on the top shelves on the left are reconditioned trade-ins.

some sell as many as five or six brands. Obviously, if you have already determined the brand you want to buy, going to a store that sells only that kind of machine is not going to be a problem. If you are comparing brands, however, a multibrand dealer seems like the most convenient option. After all, you get one-stop shopping.

But if you calculate that there may be five or more models for each of the brands (not including sergers), you could find yourself in a shop facing a bewildering number of machines, features, price points, and options. Sometimes less is more.

You would also think that a multibrand dealer is a neutral party that is going to give you "just the facts, ma'am" about all the machines. This is not likely to happen because multibrand dealers know that showing too many machines can confuse a customer and lose a sale, and dealers make

Creative Sewing Centers have seven stores in the Twin Cities market and carry six brands of machines. The selection can be overwhelming if you don't have something specific in mind; it is not a good idea to try too many machines during any one visit.

more money selling some brands than others.

Manufacturers are pretty smart in the way they set up dealership networks. They reward high-volume shops and shops that agree to carry their brands to the exclusion of others. Authorized dealers have priority over unauthorized dealers, and high-volume shops are given deeper wholesale discounts and first shipments of the new models. At annual dealer conventions held by

each company, the goal is to instill brand loyalty and selling enthusiasm in the troops on the sales front. High-volume sellers are rewarded with plaques and trophies just like at the Academy Awards.

Many brand names may be mentioned in an ad, but that doesn't mean the dealer sells them; it means he can repair them. Call the dealer to find out what new machines he is authorized to sell and what used machines he has on the shelf.

How to choose a dealer

Here's how to choose a dealer systematically.

1. Decide on what brand(s) you will consider after looking at ads, studying brochures, and talking to your sewing friends.
2. Ask your friends where they bought their machines. Were they happy with the service?
3. Call or e-mail the manufacturer (see Sewing Machine Sources on p. 102) to get the location and telephone number of the dealer nearest you. Also ask for the next nearest dealership. Try to get the names of three places.
4. Look in the Yellow Pages to identify the shops in your area that sell the brand you want. Write down the names and numbers.
5. Call each of these shops to ask for information without obligation. Here's a checklist:
   - Do you carry X brand?
   - Do you carry the full range of models of X brand?
   - Are you an authorized dealer of X brand?
   - What other brands, if any, do you carry?
   - How long have you been in business?
   - May I have the names and telephone numbers of some customers?
   - How do I get to your shop?
   - When is a good time of day to visit so that I will get your full attention?
6. If you have any doubts about a dealership, call the Better Business Bureau in your area and ask if there have been any complaints against the dealer.

Visiting the shop

The first time you visit a sewing-machine shop, I suggest you leave your cash, checkbook, and credit card at home. That simple act dramatically changes the nature of your visit by taking the pressure of making a quick and regretful decision off your shoulders. Now you can relax and concentrate on selecting the machine that is right for you.

Spend enough time in the shop to make note of the following:
- Is the shop neat, clean, and well organized? Your machine will be serviced here. If the shop is a mess, what can you expect?
- How were you greeted? Did a staff person greet you when you came into the shop? Was her tone of voice pleasant and helpful without being pushy?

- How does the dealer talk to others in the shop or on the phone? Does the dealer pay attention to you once you tell her that you left your checkbook home? When she answers the phone, does she give the person on the other end the bum's rush? That could be you on the phone with a question. Think about it.
- Are you comfortable? Do you like the person you are dealing with or does she give you the creeps? Remember that you will have to bring your machine back to this place and this person if anything goes wrong.
- If there is another customer in the shop, listen to what the dealer tells her. This is valuable information for when it is your turn. I once entered a shop bypassing a leaving customer. The last words the dealer said to her were "Give me a call when you are ready to write that check and I'll make sure you get the price you wanted." I knew immediately that this was a smart dealer willing to deal. (And I knew that I had just walked past a pretty sharp customer!)

Tricks of the trade

Most sewing-machine dealers are very honorable people. But they are honorable, *human* people, and they sometimes get carried away in their attempt to pay the rent, make a quota, or win the company award for best sales of the month. An informed shopper is a smart shopper. Here are some "tricks" to watch out for.

The last model What you will hear from a dealer: "This is the very last one of these beautiful machines that I have in stock. The new ones won't be in for months because there is such a back order on them. If you take this one off the floor, I'll give it to you at the demo-model price. It's just like new. Why, I just took it out of the box yesterday. It might not be here tomorrow."

This technique forces you to make a decision on the spot because you may lose a bargain if you don't.

I was hanging out in a dealership once when I heard the "last one" pitch. The pressure was on for the customer to make a decision right then, and she did. She bought the machine. After she walked out the door, the dealer went into the stockroom and brought out a brand-new duplicate. She had plenty of the machines in the back room.

Bait and switch How often have you seen ads in the paper advertising something wonderful for practically nothing? You walk into the store and the model that was advertised has been sold out. But, conveniently, there just happens to be a few left of a more expensive model, and they happen to be on sale. Lucky you.

What you will hear: "Oh, we had so many of them yesterday, they just flew out of the door like hotcakes. But since you came all this way, let me show you a machine that I think is a better buy. You know, because I work here I can get a great buy on any of the models on the floor. This is the one that I chose for myself."

Walk out.

Extended warranty When I bought a shop vacuum not too long ago, the salesman asked me if I wanted to buy an extended warranty for it.

This is what I heard: "For just $49.95 more, you will have extra protection just in case something breaks. You just never know. And if something does break, you will be covered. Frankly, I think it's worth the peace of mind. And you will get unlimited dust bags for three years. Just bring the old one in any time and I'll personally exchange it for a new one. Be sure to ask for me."

My answer to this $50 rip-off was this: "Well, why should something new break? And if it breaks and you are the good dealer you say you are,

why won't you stand behind your products?"

Most sewing machines are already covered for two years of parts and labor. Put that $50 in your bank account. By the time your machine needs repair, you will have money in the bank to cover the expense.

Overstock of school models The dealer says that the manufacturer made too many school machines and our warehouse is full. Out they go at just $299.99. What you will see is an ad with a photo of a school model.

There is no such thing as a school model. There are only models that manufacturers sell to schools. The implication is that these machines are built in some special way (with titanium parts, perhaps?) to with-stand the abuse of roughneck teenagers. But it's just another way to get you into the store. Don't fall for it.

On sale One sewing-machine dealership in my city has had the same sale sign in the window for three years. What kind of a sale is that? Answer: It isn't a sale at all.

What you will hear: "You are so lucky because we just happen to be running a special on these machines right now. The regular price is X but for this week it's only…."

Do you know that, like car dealers, sewing-machine dealers really have a little blue book of trade-in prices? Published by Bobette Industries, Inc. of Atlanta, it is meant to legitimize the amount of money the dealer will give you for the machine you are trading in.

If your trade-in is a junker, the dealer may give you $10 or $20 for it, then throw it in the dumpster or cannibalize it for repair parts; it's of no real use to him. If it is a machine that he can resell, he will offer you about one-quarter to one-half of what he can sell it for. After all, the dealer has to spend time cleaning and repairing your old machine and he has bills to pay. These trade-ins are the used machines you will see on any dealer's shelf when you visit the shop.

When you go into the store, the dealer will show you the suggested retail price and the price you can buy it for. The price you can buy it for *is* the real price. The other price is make-believe. Use the Yellow Pages to call other dealers to find out how much the machine you want is selling for. Sewing machines do go on sale from time to time, especially when new models are about to be introduced and when the dealer is willing to take less of a profit in order to pay the rent.

Special deal with trade-in Even well-established, national-chain department stores run sales using this popular gimmick: "Bring us any old iron and get this new one at X price." That's when everybody runs to Goodwill and buys irons for a couple of dollars so that they have something to trade in. Then, all those traded-in irons are just thrown in the dumpster or given to charity, just where they came from. I guess merchants know that you can't get something for nothing, so they ask for something, even if it's garbage.

In the case of sewing-machine dealers, they might actually receive a machine or two that they can fix up for resale. But most of their machines go in the dumpster, too.

How to bargain
There is a trend to remove bargaining from the marketplace. Car dealerships—even used-car places—tout a friendly, no-negotiation atmosphere where the buyer can be confident she is getting

the best deal possible. The price on the sticker is the price you pay.

Phooey.

First of all, I don't believe it. Second, bargaining is fun and not that difficult to do if you practice a few basic behaviors and principles, most of which you already know (what parent has never bargained with a child—if you eat your spinach, you get dessert). Here are some bargaining tips.

- Pleasant bargaining—what I call bantering bargaining—is better than hard-nosed dickering. They say honey attracts more flies than vinegar; you don't have look mean, think mean, or act mean to bargain.

- Put time on your side. You lose bargaining advantage if you are in a hurry—that's why a quick-stop shop can charge you a fortune for a Chapstick. You need it and you need it now, and you will pay what they ask.

  If you have time to make two trips to the shop, you will show that you are serious and that you will not be rushed into a deal. (On the other hand, too many visits will just annoy the dealer and may destroy your chances of getting a good deal.)

- Never show too much enthusiasm for the item you want—it makes the price go up. If you want that sewing machine so badly, why should the dealer negotiate? Be enthusiastic in your heart, not on your face.

- Be pretty sure you know what you want, but be flexible. You've done your homework, but be open to something new, something you hadn't heard about, or some new model that wasn't in the brochure. It costs you nothing to think about something. Be focused on what you want to buy, but be ready to deviate from your script if it is to your advantage to do so.

- You can negotiate a better price in a competitive market, so get prices from other dealers in the area. Sometimes there is only one dealer in your area that carries the machine you want—a disadvantage to you. Are you willing to travel to save some bucks?

- It is easier to get a better deal if you create a package. Buying a sewing machine, serger, and accessories will get you the best deal. Sometimes the "deal" isn't in the form of a discount but in a "free" accessory. The question is do you need the accessory? If you don't, it's no deal at all.

- One of the 10 commandments of negotiating is that the seller always moves down and the buyer always moves up from the opening bids. But how do you know where to start the bidding?

If you don't mention a specific model, one of the first things a merchant will casually ask you is "how much do you want to spend?" Or the merchant will say, "The price of this machine is $1,200. How much do you want to give me for this machine? You tell me the price." You think, "I'm the buyer and *I* get to set the price? Cool."

Don't fall for it. By answering this question, you tell the merchant what you know about the market (did you call around to find out what the competition is offering?), what you are willing to spend, and where she should start her bid. There is one thing you can count on: she will *always* start above your amount and work her way toward the figure you gave.

If, on the other hand, the merchant gives you her "best" price first ("What's your rock-bottom price on this machine that is marked $1,500?"), then you know where to start: You will *always* start below the amount she gave you and work your way up.

The key to good bargaining is to find out where the other person's starting point is before you reveal your own. Smile, be friendly, but never make the first offer.

- Don't make a ridiculous offer. If something is worth, say, $2,000 on the market, offering $300 for it is ridiculous. This tells the dealer that you don't know what you are doing and gives her the advantage.
- Offer something to the merchant besides your money. Buyers mistakenly think that dealers are only interested in money. The best merchants are interested in money, but they are more interested in running a good business. That means they want good, satisfied, pleasant customers like you. They enjoy customers with a good sense of humor and playfulness (it can get pretty boring fixing old sewing machines all day). You can offer the dealer your goodwill by making it clear that you intend to spread the word about the good service and good price you received from her. Offer to be a reference for the dealer, remembering that you, yourself, asked for references when you called the shop.
- Once you begin to negotiate, you are in a serious business relationship. It is up to you to do your homework, negotiate wisely,

and accept the outcome. To do otherwise is uncivilized.

For example, if you say to a dealer, "I'll give you $100 for that machine," and the dealer agrees, it is poor form (to say the least) to back out and say, "Oh, I changed my mind. I'll give you $80." A dealer to whom you do this will never give you good service or a good price because you will never be a satisfied customer no matter what she does.

How to pay for your new machine

Once you and the dealer have agreed on a price, there are a number of ways you can pay for your new machine. Here are some pros and cons of the types of payment methods.

Paying with cash When I go to garage sales, I always take plenty of cash along, never mind that writing a check is easier. The reason I do this is simple: Sellers will take less if you're paying with cash rather than a check.

Let's say you find a plate that you want to buy that's marked $7. If you hold out a five-dollar bill to the seller while you say, "Will you take five dollars for it?" I bet you will get that plate for five bucks!

There is something about the sight of hard cash that excites a seller and causes him to take it while he's got it, even if it's a bit less than he wanted. Checks, after all, can bounce.

Many sewing-machine dealers will discount for cash sales, especially on used machines.

Paying by check Aside from convenience and the safety of not having to carry large amounts of cash, there are no other bargaining advantages that I know of to paying for a sewing machine by check. Out-of-town dealers, who may have good prices, may not accept your check, or they may require the check to clear, which could take up to two weeks, before sending you the machine.

Paying by credit card If there is no bargaining or convenience advantage in paying for something with cash, my next favorite way to pay is with a credit card. It takes 30 days for me to get the bill, and that's 30 days I can keep my money in the bank collecting interest.

Since there is no way I am going to pay a credit-card company 18% interest on my hard-earned money, I have devised a way that keeps me from spending money I don't have. I "pencil deposit" a certain amount of "money" into my credit-card account book each month (I use an extra checking-account register booklet that comes with my checks). Then when I buy on credit, I subtract the amount from my "balance." When there is not enough "money" in my "account" to cover my purchases, I don't use the credit card. It really works; this is a great way to budget your money.

Too complicated? Just cut up that credit card and destroy temptation right now. Go ahead, get the scissors.

Besides using somebody else's money for a month (banks call it a loan or a float), I used to think that credit-card purchases gave me protection against unscrupulous merchants as well. But I've discovered that isn't necessarily so.

A while ago, I bought a reconditioned used machine for $400 and paid for it by credit card. After a few weeks (and before I received the credit-card bill for that purchase), the machine started to act up and I discovered that the motor brushes where completely worn away. The merchant wouldn't take the machine back, so I called the credit-card company and asked them if they could do anything about it. The answer was a disappointing "Sorry, we can't help you with that; the purchase has already gone through the system. You'll just have to talk to the dealer."

Before you pay for that sewing machine with plastic, you may want to call your credit-card company and find out what kind of consumer protection you can expect.

Using the manufacturer's credit card

Many sewing-machine companies are tempting buyers with no-payment-'til-whenever plans that are very appealing. This is how it works: You apply for and receive the sewing-machine company's credit card. Then you charge your purchase to that card with no payments due until a certain date—usually "next year," even though that may only be three months away.

Sounds good doesn't it? Yes, it can be a great opportunity. You get to take a new sewing machine home and play with it for several months, and it didn't cost you a cent...until the clock strikes 12!

Then again, it can cost you a bundle.

The company is actually making you a short-term, no-interest loan *if* you come up with the money on the due date, when the clock strikes 12. If you don't pay the whole amount, you will start paying a huge interest on your loan. At 18% or more interest, your thousand-dollar machine is going to cost you a lot more than you ever imagined.

Take my advice: Set the full purchase price of the machine in a certificate of deposit (CD), collecting interest at 4% or 5%, that will mature when your first payment is due. Then accept the company's kind offer. When the payment is due, cash in your CD, and pay the entire bill. Use the interest money you've earned to buy an accessory for your machine, some thread, or some fabric.

Money for your old machine

Sewing-machine dealers are not going to "give" you money for your old machine unless you purchase a new one (or you are silly enough to ask for a few dollars for a machine they know they can sell for lots, lots more). They usually have more old machines than they know what to do with.

The money the merchant is going to give you is actually a reduction on the purchase of a new machine. So, I'd consider a trade-in as a form of payment: I'll give you this old machine, and you give me $250 toward my new machine. Sounds like good money to me.

Even swap Rarely, but from time to time, a dealer may be willing to swap one of his used machines for the machine you have to offer. Obviously, he isn't going to swap a good machine for a piece of junk, but he may be willing to swap something with features you like for something he likes even better. (For example, he may have a special customer that is looking for your type of machine.) Even though it's a long shot, take my mother's advice: "It doesn't hurt to ask."

Installment payments If you see a machine that you like at a price that is attractive, you can arrange with most dealers to pay for it in installments. That means that you reserve the machine while the dealer keeps it until you pay for it in full, usually in monthly or quarterly installments. The advantage to the dealer is that she puts your money in her bank account and collects interest. The advantage to you is that you lock in the price. If the prices go up, which is likely, you win. If the prices go down as they might in a model closeout, for example, you lose. Personally, I don't like to buy stuff if I don't have the money.

CHAPTER FIVE

Smart Ways to Use a Sewing Machine

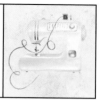

You have done a lot of work deciding, choosing, and bargaining, and now the machine is yours. You would think this book should end here with a simple and sincere "Happy sewing!"

Well, it's because I *do* wish you happy sewing that I've written this chapter. I want you to get the most out of your machine and the most out of your sewing hobby; bringing your li'l darlin' home is just the beginning.

WHEN YOU GET YOUR MACHINE HOME

No matter how old I get, there are few things that excite me more than a new toy. So I'm not going to tell you to keep your new sewing machine in the box for a few days while you carefully read the manual. The first thing I want you to do is have fun.

I want you to plug that hummer in and play, play, play with it for a while. Touch it. Kiss it. Smile to your lucky, deserving self. Step on the "gas" pedal and listen to the sound of your new machine. (Remember that sound; when it changes, something's wrong.) Invite a friend over for coffee and show off. Play with the buttons and knobs (you can't do any harm if there is no thread in the machine).

Next, to turn your new toy into a wonderful creative tool, you must read that manual. In fact, don't read it, study it. Go through its pages front to back; the time you spend now will come back to you in fewer headaches and repairs, fewer trips to the dealer (only to have her say the solution to the problem is on page 9), and better sewing.

Use the manual

Sewing-machine manufacturers are so determined to give you the best-engineered, best-designed sewing appliance that they often neglect an important part of the machine: the instruction manual. That's too bad because good instructions can make your experience with the machine a dream come true, while poorly written, confusing instructions can plunge you into a frustrating tangle that has you wondering why you bought the darned thing, or worse, why you thought sewing was going to be relaxing and fun.

Manuals are not easy to write. As sewing machines get more complicated, the instruction books get thicker. Think for a moment about what has to go into one: safety instructions, setup information, first-time-sewer information, maintenance information, "what if..." charts about what could go wrong, advanced sewing techniques, creative ideas, needle and thread charts, and instructions on how to use various attachments like feet, cutters, buttonholers, and guides. Now imagine that all of this has to be done in several languages for various world markets, and a manual becomes a mighty big project.

When you are shopping for a machine, make sure that you consider the manual as part of your purchase. Look it over before you

buy the machine and see if it makes sense. If it looks poorly written but you are determined to buy the machine, ask the dealer if he has supplementary materials (from the company or from his own teaching staff) that will help clarify things. He may be willing to throw some of these guides into the bargain.

Lastly, approach the manual systematically. Even though you may be an experienced sewer, take the time to read the manual from cover to cover at least once.

One more suggestion: If the manual is really unhelpful to you, write to the company and complain. Who knows, they may hire you to write the next one!

Test your machine

All sewing machines are tested before they leave the factory, and you should test the machine before it leaves the dealership where you bought it. Chances are your machine will work perfectly.

If there is anything wrong with your machine, you will want to know about it in the first few days you have it. That is why I suggest you try it—try all of it—during those first few days. Work your way through the manual and see that everything is functioning as promised.

Leave computerized machines turned on for 24 hours. In that time, you will know if any of the chips are faulty. If the machine functions well for a few days, chances are that not much is going to go wrong with it.

Recognize that this machine isn't going to do things the way your old one did. That's normal. You have to learn some new things even if you are a veteran sewer. If there is something that isn't functioning properly, read the "what if..." section of the manual to see if you missed a step or did something "the old way." If you can't correct the problem, report any irregularities to the dealer.

Sign up for classes

Dealers know that you will not be a happy customer if you don't know how to use your sewing machine properly and to its capacity. That is why they offer classes with every machine they sell. The first class, which is the introduction to your machine, is usually free. In other words, the class was part of your purchase. Go to the class.

No instruction manual can cover all aspects of sewing or predict all the questions you might have. The education staff is prepared to show you some of the basics and many techniques and shortcuts that are not covered in the manual. Since these instructors use the machines every day and they are in contact with lots of sewers, they have a lot of useful information. They also know the weak or frustrating points of the machine (every machine has some), and they know how to work around them.

Since you have to bring your new machine to these classes, it is a perfect time and setting to clear things up if there is any malfunction or feature that you don't understand.

Make a stitch dictionary

I strongly suggest that you make samples of the stitches illustrated in the manual and then paste or staple them into the book or keep them on a handy strip of material as I do. No matter how much I sew, nothing is more helpful to me than a look at an actual sample of the stitch or technique I'm about to use. (No illustration of a stitch can match a sewn-out sample; you are going to be surprised at how different some stitches look. It's better to be surprised on the sample than on an important project.) And don't be afraid to write in the manual's margins, especially to note when you change the recommended settings to ones you like better.

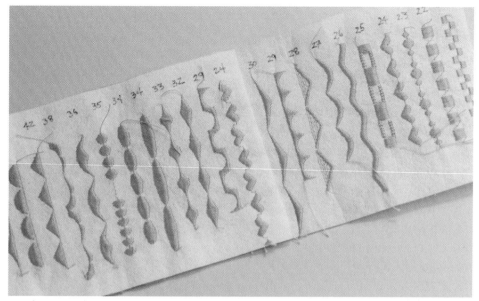

Neither a sophisticated computer screen nor documentation with photos, graphs, and drawings can convey to you what a stitch is really going to look like, so it's best to sew stitches out on a strip of stiff material and keep them at hand.

When to call the dealer

Yes, you may call your dealer or salesperson to do more than complain! You can call just to say hello. (Have you hugged your sewing-machine dealer lately? Seriously, the sewing-machine business is tough, and most of these people do a very good job serving the various needs of the sewing community.)

You can also call for information that isn't connected to a complaint. For example, call for news of new accessories or computer-design cards for your machine or for schedules of upcoming classes and needlework shows in town.

And, of course, your dealer is there to help you with the problems you are having with your machine, if not with your sewing project itself.

Before you call the dealer with a technical question, look toward the end of your manual for a "what if…" section. Read that section and you will probably solve your problem. If you don't have a "what if…" section in your manual, here's my advice:

1. Stop! Stop what you are doing. Shut the machine off. Go into

another room and have a cup of tea or chop some onions with a sharp knife. (That always takes my mind off of unsavory things like machines that won't cooperate.)

2. After a while, you will come back to your machine with "new eyes" and renewed patience. Unplug the machine to show it that you are in charge.

3. Unthread the machine. Take out the bobbin and check to see that it is wound properly and is turning in the right direction. Reinstall it carefully. Rethread the machine, carefully following the instructions in the manual. Make sure the thread falls into all of the proper channels and catches as illustrated.

4. Change the needle. Or, if it's brand new, reinstall the needle, making sure it is facing the correct direction. Even a new needle can be defective. Thread it in the correct direction (usually front to back on new machines but often otherwise on older machines, so check the manual).

5. Say nice things out loud. Plug the machine in and turn it on.

6. Sew something. If it doesn't sew properly, stop. Unplug the machine and repeat steps 3 to 5. If it still doesn't work, then call the dealer. She will either help you over the phone or tell you to bring the machine in for an inspection. Good service includes helping reasonable customers get the most out of their machines.

Please don't become one of those people dealers call an RTFMS (read the fabulous manual, stupid). I once was visiting a local dealer and his repairman when there were no customers in the shop. In the middle of our conversation, for reasons I couldn't figure out, the repairman quickly disappeared into his workroom and the dealer started acting busy. They had spied Mrs. X parking in front of the store and heading toward the front door. When she left, they returned to normal and explained that Mrs. X was a constant and annoying visitor who kept asking the same fundamental questions over and over again but refused to read the manual or go to any of the free classes they offered. "We are sorry we sold her a machine," they said.

Call the dealer with *good* questions and to learn new and exciting things. Don't waste her service and goodwill on things you could have looked up quickly. You'd be surprised how much more you will get from a dealer if she considers you a pleasant, intelligent, and reasonable customer.

When to call the manufacturer

Most manufacturers have sewing-education and technical departments staffed by expert, friendly people who know the ins and outs of sewing and all the machines in the line. They are there to support dealers, who in turn support you, the consumer. One of the members of this team is the customer relations representative who talks directly to customers (by phone or, increasingly, via the Internet) when the dealer cannot or will not help. Her goal is to try to keep you on good terms with your dealer, but she will intervene if the dealer is unwilling or unable to help you.

If there is something wrong with your machine, it is always best to return it to the dealer from whom you bought it. It will just confuse the manufacturer if you ship the machine back to the head office; the manufacturer will just ship it back to you and tell you to bring it to your local dealer (and you've wasted a lot of sewing days). If your local dealer can't fix your machine, she will send it to the home office for repair. Be forewarned, however, that a sewing machine is like an automobile: once you buy it, it is yours. It is unusual for a dealer to replace a machine rather than fix the problem. If there is something *seriously* wrong, however, and the machine is just a few days old, the dealer may send it back to the factory and give you a new one.

SETTING UP YOUR SEWING SPACE

Let's be positive and assume that you have taken your new machine out of the box, tested it, and everything is fine. We are now ready to talk about the best ways to set up your machine for productive, creative sewing.

Sewing is like cooking in that you don't need a lot of fancy equipment to do the job, but the job is best done with good ingredients and under the right conditions. In both cases, time, place, space, lighting, noise, temperature, and energy needs are all important factors.

I am astounded at how many sewers invest thousands of dollars in a great appliance and proceed to use it in the most uncomfortable and unproductive places. One person I know constantly complains of back problems when she sews, and no wonder! She is sitting on a dining-room chair in poor light, with her feet barely touching the floor and her body leaning to one side because the table leg is in her way. After a few hours of this torture, I'm surprised she can sew anything. Here are a few suggestions for how to improve your sewing situation.

When to sew

These days a lot of us have to "steal" time to sew. This could be on weekends, in the evenings, in front of the TV, or when the kids are taking a nap or in school. Some people like to sew during the day to take advantage of natural light.

Since there is no TV in my house, after-dinner together-time is when my family and I all "do" something. It's the perfect time to capture an hour or two for sewing, but those are not entirely uninterrupted hours. Most of the time, I like people around when I sew, but you may not. It's a personal thing. And, of course, it depends on the project. If I'm mending a shirt, I can do it in front of anyone, but don't disturb me when I'm cutting out the fabric. (I always try to do that part in the morning, when the house is quiet and I'm really focused.)

When you sew may determine where you sew. For example, if you enjoy sewing until midnight, sewing in the bedroom might not be possible if your partner is in bed by 10.

Where to sew

I've seen sewing "rooms" in the oddest places, and quite frankly, if an odd place works for you, what does it matter whether you are sewing in a closet, a corner in your bedroom, the kitchen, the basement playroom, or a new skylighted sewing studio? Your grandmother's sewing place was anywhere she took her old fruitcake tin containing her few sewing supplies.

Wherever you decide to sew and whatever your budget and space constraints, I recommend one thing: Try to have your machine out and ready to use at all times. There is no greater damper of sewing enthusiasm than to have to set up your sewing "room" every time you want to sew. No matter where your sewing place is, try to make it permanent.

I know a woman who does not have a permanent place in her house to sew, so she keeps her sewing machine and supplies on a sturdy rolling cart and moves the machine where she needs to. That way the machine is always out and her

Every sewer's needs are different, but here's an arrangement I like a lot: The sewing machine is on an adjustable computer table to make sewing comfortable. The table on the left is on wheels so it can slide to the bed of the machine to give me a huge sewing surface. The architect's taboret on the right, also on wheels, holds thread, feet, and pieces of my current project.

sewing room is wherever the cart goes. If she can roll her cart up to the dining-room table, she has a huge surface to work on. If the kids are all over the table, she can take her cart into the bedroom or into the kitchen. Sewing in the guest bathroom, anyone?

Your sewing space

Where you sew (place) is one thing. The organization of the area around you as you sew (space) is another. The most important spaces in your sewing place are the ones around your machine and ironing board.

I have spent a lot of time organizing the area around my sewing machine so that I can sew efficiently and comfortably (see the photo above). Since the area to the left of the machine must be clear for the sewing project itself, it is the small area to the right and front of the machine that holds my thread snips, seam ripper, and extra filled bobbins. If you have the space, an architect's taboret or similar catchall is perfect to have at your right hand. It is out of your sewing way and holds all the sewing-machine equipment you need.

I like to put my sewing machine on a carpet square; it makes the machine quieter, and I can put small items like bobbins and a seam ripper on it so they won't roll off the table. Another tip is to tie one end of string around the thread snips and the other end to your sewing machine or the table leg, so you will never run around your sewing room or house looking for them again. (Of course, you can tie them around your neck and they will follow you everywhere, but I consider scissors dangling in front of me as I sew annoying if not dangerous.)

While you can cut fabric any time and on any large, flat surface, you cannot really place your ironing board too far from your sewing machine and consider yourself a sewer. The two skills go hand in hand. If you are a quilter, you know that you do just as much ironing as sewing, and if you are making garments, ironing and pressing are crucial to professional-looking results. For these reasons, you want your ironing board close to your sewing machine. But don't plug the sewing machine and iron into the same outlet if you can help it; irons use a lot of energy, and this may affect the performance of your sewing machine.

Lighting

Nothing is more critical to accurate sewing than the precise guiding of fabric through the machine with your eye and hand. This requires you to keep your eye on the needle or the edge of the sewing foot, but how can you do that if you can't see well?

Even the best built-in sewing-machine lights are not adequate for comfortable sewing. They are dim, cast shadows across the needle, or create a strobe effect of rapidly alternating light and shadow as the needle goes up and down that is enough to give anyone a headache.

Place your machine near a window (north facing is best) if you sew during the daytime. Place your sewing table so the window is to your left and the light pours across the needle and your project. If you have to have a shadow, let it fall to the right, away from the needle area.

Buy a gooseneck or drafting-table lamp and clamp it behind and to the left of your machine to supplement the lighting on dark days or when sewing in darker places. While the bases of these lamps are fixed, the lamps are designed to stretch and direct the light where you need it most. If you don't have room on the table for the light, buy one of the '50s funky pole lamps at the Salvation Army. Put it in front of your sewing table next to your left arm, and aim one of the lights at the needle area.

Since I like to have some lighting to the right of my needle, I find that one of those little book lights does a great job. It's small, flexible, and provides just enough light to make a difference. There are some interesting flexible, snake-like lamps on the market these days. The ones I have seen are battery powered, which would eliminate the problem of a power supply and cord.

For overall shadow-free room lighting, nothing beats a 300-watt halogen light that is aimed at the ceiling (the light's too bright to aim it directly at the machine, and it hurts the eyes if you look at it directly). These inexpensive lamps are available at home centers for less than $20 and come in clip-on, short-stand, and taller tripod models.

Noise

I usually have the radio on when I'm sewing, but I can't tolerate it at all when I am writing. Is sewing a quiet, contemplative activity for you? Or do you like to sew to Abba? Do you want to answer the phone when you are in the middle of a sewing project, or do you let the answering machine get it?

In general, sewing equipment is pretty quiet unless you are using it. Some brands are very quiet, while some are real noisemakers with shrill beeps and rough-sounding motors. Remember that a machine will sound twice as loud at home as it was in the busy shop. In general, the top-of-the-line machines are quieter than the cheaper models, but even top-of-the-line machines can differ greatly in the amount of noise they make. (If you are a fanatic about noises, get a used Elna Carina made in the 1970s. It remains one of the quietest machines ever made.)

I have an older machine that wasn't as quiet as I would have liked, so I pasted craft felt in every internal place where it wouldn't interfere with the operation of the machine (see the photo on p. 92). I lined the bobbin door and the internal spaces adjacent to the foot. The top of the machine comes off, so I was able to paste felt up there too, using a UHU glue stick. The result was an unsightly patchwork of ugly felt, but it was inside the machine, visible to no one, and I reduced the noise by almost half. If

If your machine is noisy even after you've cleaned and oiled it, consider pasting some felt on inside surfaces to absorb the sound. Make sure the felt is secure and doesn't interfere with any moving parts.

you try this, just make sure you do a good job of gluing the pieces to clean surfaces of the machine; you don't want that felt to pop off and get caught in the sewing mechanism. Check it once in a while to see that it is secure. To further reduce the machine's noise level, put the machine on a carpet square.

Temperature and moisture
It's funny how temperature becomes more important to you as you get older.

My sewing room and office is in the lower level—let's be honest, it's the basement—of my house. The room has full-length windows because the house sits on an inclined lot, but it's still a basement. In the summer the dehumidifier extracts a few gallons of water out of the air every day, and in winter an extra heater is necessary.

Here's how I handle this less-than-ideal situation: In the summer I garden instead of sew. If I have to go into the sewing room, I wait for clear, humidity-free days and open the windows or I turn off the noisy dehumidifier.

In fall and winter when I really start sewing big time, I prepare the room for comfort a half hour before I actually start sewing. I turn on the space heater if needed and the lights on the machines I intend to use. Sewing machines are no different than your car (and you for that matter): They are sluggish when they are cold. The metal and the lubrication in the machines need to warm up before they will run smoothly. The little light inside the machine is enough to warm it up, especially if you keep the machine covered with a piece of cloth. (I always cover my machines with a piece of fabric to keep the dust and grit off of them anyway. Don't use plastic because it traps moisture, an enemy of sewing machines.) After a half hour of sitting under the heated "tent," the machine is ready to use no matter what the temperature is in the rest of the room.

Because my feet and hands get cold and stiff in the winter, I make sure that I don't sew on an empty stomach. I usually sew after fueling up at dinnertime, when I have enough carbohydrates in my body to keep me warm. Sheerling-lined, ankle-high moccasins and heavy wool socks keep my feet nice and warm on the basement floor. Moccasins don't have a stiff sole, so they are especially good at giving my foot a good feel for the sewing pedal. It's the next best thing to sewing barefoot.

It also helps to have a nonskid rug under your sewing table. The rug not only keeps your feet warmer, but it also keeps the sewing pedal from sliding around, especially if you glue Velcro strips to the pedal's bottom.

A lot of heat leaves your body through the top of your head, but most people I know would think it ridiculous to wear a hat in the house. I do wear one, and I encourage you to try it. In fact, I now make "winter house hats" for my friends. A hat is a small sewing project, and you can make decorative bands around the side with all those fancy stitches on your new machine! If you don't feel like sewing a hat, just buy and wear a Polarfleece ski cap. You will be surprised at how a hat keeps your whole body warm.

If you find that your legs get cold, cut a "folding screen" from an appliance-size cardboard box that you can put around or under your sewing table. The cardboard will keep drafts from reaching and chilling your legs, especially if you sew near a window.

Flooring

Because the floor would be cold, I didn't want to install my preference for a great, easy-to-clean, sewing-room floor: linoleum. I used commercial, low, dense-pile carpet squares instead (the kind used in airports), knowing full well that they would catch and hold threads and fabric fuzz. Actually, the electric carpet sweeper attachment for my vacuum does a great job of picking up after I've collected the longer threads by hand.

Aside from the hassle of vacuuming, there are some advantages to having the right kind of carpet in the sewing room. Not only is carpet warmer than linoleum but it also is a great no-skid cutting and prep surface for large projects. I place pins through the carpet into its rubber backing to hold the fabric or quilt in place.

If you have a linoleum or wooden floor, use a rubberized place mat (the mesh kind made for summer picnics) under the sewing pedal to keep it from sliding. I get the place mats at thrift shops for about 25 cents apiece.

Electricity

Unless you are using a treadle machine and only sew in daylight, you need electricity nearby when you sew. Sewing machines don't use a lot of energy, but an iron and a 300-watt halogen light do. As I mentioned earlier, try not to have your machine and your iron on the same circuit, especially if you are using a computerized machine. I have all my machines plugged into circuit-breaker "energy" strips so that any minor voltage irregularities will not damage my machine. But be forewarned: These strips won't keep your machine from frying during an electrical storm. When those storms happen, I unplug the electric strips so all the electrical items are unplugged at once.

THE SEWING TABLE

Grandma's flatbed sewing machine was probably set into a sewing table with a flip top that became an extended sewing surface. This concept was an excellent one, since the table was an extension of the machine itself and served to support the fabric as Grandma guided it under the needle. Unfortunately, today's machines are mostly free arm (light and portable are what the consumer wants) and are not designed to fit into a table. In my opinion, the quality of the sewing suffers because of this.

Some manufacturers, such as Bernina, do provide a small sewing table that you can attach to the free arm, which is helpful with some projects. For example, when I am chain-piecing a patchwork, that slide-on table is often large enough to handle all the little pieces. But when it comes to machine quilting, I want plenty of support all around me to hold up the queen-size-bed dimensions of the quilt.

You can support your project in a number of ways, some expensive and some that will cost you virtually nothing. Put your machine on the largest surface available. Any extension should be as level with the feed dogs as you can get.

- Make a template of the free arm of your machine and cut that shape out of the right-hand end of a flat board. You can have a local woodworker make a Formica tabletop with a cutout for your machine, or you can make one yourself out of any number of substances. For example, you can cut the free-arm shape out of a piece of plywood and fit the wood with adjustable legs that you can buy in any hardware store. Be sure to cover the wood with something

smooth like oil cloth or Con-tact paper so your fabric won't drag on the rough surface.

- Use a tabletop ironing board. I always see tabletop ironing boards made of particleboard in junk shops; you know, the 1-ft. by 2-ft. kind with the little plastic tube feet. Take off the fabric cover, and there is your extension table ready to be cut to fit your machine.

- Make a cardboard extension table. If you aren't handy with a saw and you don't want to spend the money for a deluxe surface, you can make an extension table out of cardboard (see the photo on p. 96). With a sharp X-acto knife, cut the top out of two layers of corrugated cardboard (foam-core board would also work), using a large kitchen cutting board as a template. Carefully trace an outline of the top of the free arm on a piece of typing paper, using your fingernails to score the edges. Transfer the pattern to the cardboard and carefully cut out the shape.

Next, carefully measure the distance from the base of the sewing machine to the top of the free-arm sewing surface and subtract the thickness of the cardboard you are using. Cut cardboard strips this height, then

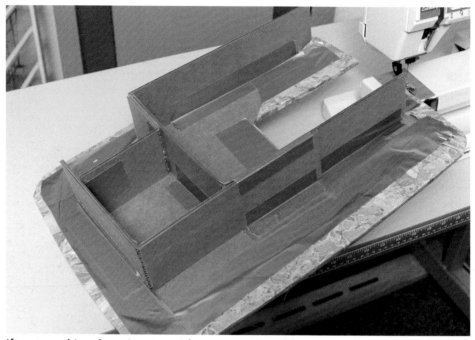

If your machine doesn't come with an extension table, you can buy a clear Plexiglas one for $60 or you can make one out of cardboard, duct tape, and Con-tact paper, as shown here.

score, bend, and tape the strips to the bottom of the extension table so that they provide good support all around and slide around the base of the machine. Cover the surface with Con-tact paper so the fabric can move without dragging. I've made these for several of my machines and they work great. Dealers sell clear Plexiglas versions of my cardboard table for more than $60.

THE CUTTING TABLE

Cutting fabric is not my favorite part of sewing. But there is one thing I dislike even more: clearing the table of all books, mail, and other stuff to make room for cutting. Before I even pick up the scissors, I'm in a bad mood.

Use the largest flat surface in your house—usually the dining room or kitchen table—for cutting fabric. Once you remove the income tax forms and the kids' homework, you

The Johnny G Tilt

Do you remember the desk you had in grade school? I bet its surface was slightly tilted toward you just like a drafting table or an old-fashioned accountant's table. That's because somebody knew that writing for long periods on a flat surface was not a very comfortable thing to do. Sewing on a flat surface isn't the most comfortable way to sew either.

Try this: Buy two 1-in. art-gum erasers and put them under the back side of your machine to tilt the machine slightly toward you (see the photo at right). The erasers will not let the machine slide around or jump into your lap. Try sewing on the tilted machine for a few hours; it will feel different, but the tilt will allow you to look down on the needle instead of across at it. It may change the way you sew.

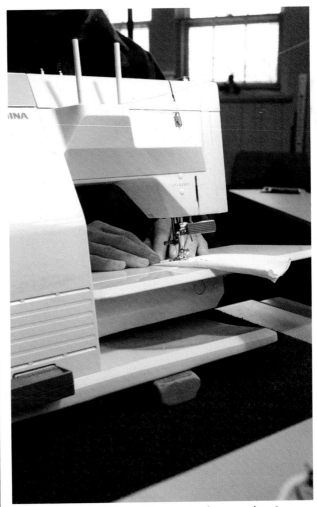

Tilting your sewing machine toward you makes it easier to see, lessens arm and eye fatigue, and improves sewing accuracy. Put two 1-in. art-gum erasers under the back bottom of your machine to tilt the machine toward you.

might be able to use it for sewing. The green felt side of protective dining-room-table pads is just about perfect for cutting. You can stick pins in it, too.

Whatever surface you use, it must be at the right height for you. I like to use the kitchen counter rule when talking about the right height of a cutting table: Do you find your kitchen counters too low to comfortably prepare food for more than a few minutes? If you have to bend over all the time, you are going to get tired, or worse, get back trouble. You can easily test this rule by placing some food on a 1-in.- to 2-in.-thick cutting board to see if the higher height feels better to you. If you find the countertop too high, place the cutting board on a bowl in the sink or on an open drawer to see how low is comfortable for you. Try cutting some vegetables at that height for a few meals to see if you like it. When you find the right height for you, measure it and make that your cutting table height.

If you have the space, here's an easy way to create a large cutting surface. Buy a standard 4-ft. by 8-ft. piece of plywood and cover it with either linoleum, if you prefer a smooth work top, or a mattress pad covered with a cotton sheet or linen tablecloth. (The tooth of the cloth covering will grab and hold your project just like the flannel or felt board used in schools. You can iron on it, too.) Set the plywood on the dining-room or kitchen table. If you need more height, place some 2x4s on the table first, then the plywood on top of that. You can also set up sawhorses to hold the plywood at the right height.

I see lots of portable cutting tables for sale in sewing magazines and wonder how you can cut on such a wobbly piece of equipment. Whatever table you use, make sure it is stable and wobble-free.

Finally, when I was working on a very large quilt, my mother-in-law suggested I use the floor. Why didn't I think of that? If the carpet is thin enough (like the commercial carpeting I have in my sewing room, for example), you can even stick pins in it. Just get down on your hands and knees and get to work!

YOUR SEWING CHAIR

Since sewing is a seated activity, a good sewing chair set to the proper height is a must for the serious sewer.

Most people sit in chairs that are set too high for them. The height of your sewing chair depends on your size—more specifically, on the length of your legs. For comfortable sewing, you should sit in such a way that there is no pressure on the backs of your legs. You can accomplish this by lowering the chair or raising the floor under your feet.

The simplest thing to do, believe it or not, is to raise the floor under your feet. Just build up the area in front of your sewing chair with carpet squares. This way you don't have to change the height of your sewing table, something you would have to do if you lowered the chair itself. By lifting your feet, you lessen the pressure on your legs, so you can sit comfortably for hours.

The slightly more expensive alternative is to find an adjustable chair, like an office chair, and set it to the correct height. But you'll have to adjust the tabletop so that your sewing machine is at the right height, too.

I have three kinds of seats in my sewing room, and I use and like them all. If I am simply reattaching a button to a shirt or jumping from machine to machine, I will perch on a cushion-covered piano stool to do the job. It's adjustable, has wheels, and slides easily out of the way under a table or in a corner.

But if I am going to be sitting at the machine for a long time (to chain-sew patchwork pieces, for

The top of this typical sewing cabinet is 31 in. off the floor, far too high for my 5-ft. 7-in. height. The standard kitchen chair is also too high. It puts pressure on the back of my upper legs, cutting off circulation. I have to lean forward to see what I am sewing, which is not good for my back.

Sewing Comfort

The proper height chair and table are essential for stress-free sewing. The illustration on the left shows incorrect posture, which can lead to pressure on the neck, back, legs, and wrists. The illustration on the right shows the proper way to set up your sewing area to eliminate stress. Your height determines comfort; select the chair first, then the table.

INCORRECT POSTURE

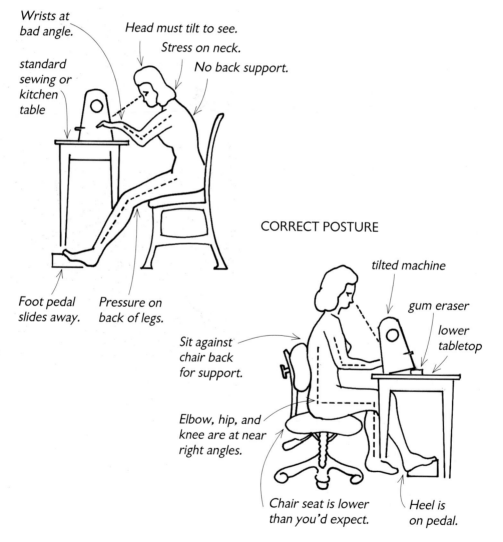

Wrists at bad angle.

Head must tilt to see.

Stress on neck.

No back support.

standard sewing or kitchen table

Foot pedal slides away.

Pressure on back of legs.

CORRECT POSTURE

tilted machine

gum eraser

lower tabletop

Sit against chair back for support.

Elbow, hip, and knee are at near right angles.

Chair seat is lower than you'd expect.

Heel is on pedal.

example), I need back support so I use a good, armless office chair, sometimes called a secretary's or typing chair. Like the piano stool, this chair also has wheels and adjustable height. In addition, I can adjust the tension and height of the form-fitting back to fit my posture and sewing needs.

My advice is to buy the best office chair you can afford since you are going to be sitting in it for long periods of time. Your back is worth it. Since businesses are always upgrading their office furniture, you can get good deals on posture-friendly chairs in secondhand office-furniture supply stores. Look in the Yellow Pages under used office furniture. When you go to the office-furniture store, be prepared to see scores of models to choose from. (While you are there, look at desks that can make good sewing tables and shelving that can hold your fabric.)

The third chair in my sewing room is the one I call the finishing chair. When I'm ripping a seam, doing handwork, or simply watching the embroidery machine do its thing, I like to "lounge" in this chair. It has supportive arms that I could never tolerate when I'm at a sewing machine.

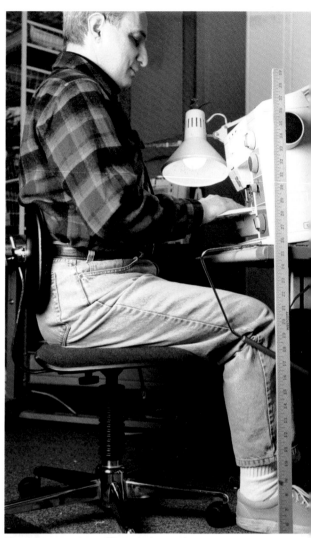

The inexpensive office chair can be raised and lowered so that my legs are almost at right angles to my body. There is little pressure on the backs of my legs. The adjustable tabletop is set at 26 in., which brings the sewing surface to 29 in., a comfortable height for me.

Sewing Machine Sources

Baby Lock
Baby Lock USA
PO Box 730
Fenton, MO 63026-9946
(800) 422-2952
website: http://www.babylock.
com

Bernette, Bernina
Bernina of America
3500 Thayer Ct.
Aurora, IL 60504-6182
(800) 405-2739
website: http://www.berninausa.
com

Bernina Canada
660 Denison St.
Markham, ON L3R 1C1 Canada
(905) 475-9365

Brother
Brother International
200 Cottontail Ln.
Somerset, NJ 08875-6174
(800) 284-4357
website: http://www.brother.com

Brother Canada
1 Rue Hotel de Ville
Dollard-des-Ormeaux, QB
   H9B 3H6 Canada
(514) 685-0604, ext. 233

Elna, Elnita
Elna USA
1760 Gilsinn Ln.
Fenton, MO 63026
(800) 848-3562

Husqvarna, Viking, White
Husqvarna/Viking/White Sewing
   Machine Co.
VWS Service Center
11760 Berea Rd.
Cleveland, OH 44111
(800) 446-2333
website: http://www.
   husqvarnaviking.com

Kenmore

Sears Roebuck Co.
3333 Beverly Rd.
Hoffman Estates, IL 60179
Contact your local Sears store.
website: http://www.sears.com

Necchi

Allyn International
1075 Santa Fe Dr.
Denver, CO 80204
(800) 525-9987
website: http://www.allynint.com

New Home

New Home Sewing Machine Co.
10 Industrial Ave.
Mahwah, NJ 07430
(800) 631-0183
website: http://www2.gol.com/
   users/janome01

New Home Sewing Machine Co.
   (Canada)
Unit 3, 6620 Kitimat Rd.
Mississauga, ON L5N 2B8
   Canada
(905) 821-0266

Pfaff

Pfaff America
610 Winters Ave.
Paramus, NJ 07653-0566
(800) 997-3233, (800) 363-0786
   (Canada)
website: http://www.pfaff.com

Riccar

Riccar Sewing Machines
1800 E. Walnut Ave.
Fullerton, CA 92831
(800) 995-9110

Simplicity

Simplicity Sewing Machines
1760 Gilsinn Ln.
Fenton, MO 63026
(800) 335-0025

Singer

Singer Sewing Co.
4500 Singer Rd.
Murfreesboro, TN 37130
(800) 877-7762
website: http://www.
   singersewing.com

Index

Book publisher: **Jim Childs**

Acquisitions editor: **Jolynn Gower**

Publishing coordinator: **Sarah Coe**

Editor: **Diane Sinitsky**

Designer: **Lynne Phillips**

Layout artist/illustrator: **Rosalie Vaccaro**

Photographer: **Boyd Hagen**

Typeface: **Horley Old Style, Avenir**

Paper: **70-lb. Somerset Matte**

Printer: **R. R. Donnelley, Willard, Ohio**